THE GRAPES OF WRATH

THE GRAPES OF WRATH

Adapted by Tim Baker
Based on the novel by John Steinbeck

JOSEF WEINBERGER PLAYS

LONDON

First published in 2008
by Josef Weinberger Ltd
12-14 Mortimer Street, London, W1T 3JJ
www.josef-weinberger.com
general.info@jwmail.co.uk

Copyright © 2008 by Tim Baker
Copyright © 2006 as an unpublished dramatic composition by Tim Baker

The author asserts his moral right to be identified as the author of the work.

ISBN   978 0 85676 320 5 (13 digit)

This play is protected by Copyright. According to Copyright Law, no public performance or reading of a protected play or part of that play may be given without prior authorisation from Josef Weinberger Plays, as agent for the Copyright Owners.

From time to time it is necessary to restrict or even withdraw the rights of certain plays. **It is therefore essential to check with us before making a commitment to produce a play.**

NO PERFORMANCE MAY BE GIVEN WITHOUT A LICENCE

AMATEUR PRODUCTIONS

Royalties are due at least one calendar month prior to the first performance. A royalty quotation will be issued upon receipt of the following details:

Name of Licensee
Play Title
Place of Performance
Dates and Number of Performances
Audience Capacity
Ticket Prices

PROFESSIONAL PRODUCTIONS

All enquiries regarding professional rights should be addressed to Josef Weinberger Ltd at the address above.

OVERSEAS PRODUCTIONS

Applications for productions overseas should be addressed to our local authorised agents. Further details are listed in our catalogue of plays, published every two years, or available from Josef Weinberger Plays at the address above.

CONDITIONS OF SALE

This book is sold subject to the condition that it shall not by way of trade or otherwise be resold, hired out, circulated or distributed without prior consent of the Publisher. **Reproduction of the text either in whole or part and by any means is strictly forbidden.**

SPECIAL NOTE ON MUSIC

Please contact Josef Weinberger for information regarding the use of Dyfan Jones' original score.

Printed in England by Commercial Colour Press plc, Hainault, Essex

THE GRAPES OF WRATH was first produced by Clwyd Theatr Cymru at the Antony Hopkins Theatre, Mold, Clwyd on 14th September 2006.

The Company

Catrin Aaron, John Biggins, John Cording, Bradley Freegard, Lynn Hunter, Maldwyn John, Gwyn Vaughan Jones, Rhys Parry Jones, Garry Lake, Lee Mengo, Jane Milligan, Dyfrig Morris, Simon Nehan, Wendy Parkin, Lucy Rivers, Clêr Stephens.

Children
(Two teams of nine, playing alternate nights.)

Molly Austen, Ashley Cartwright, Eleanore Custance, Abigail Davies-Moore, Sophie Downes, Shay Griffiths, Matthew Grosart, Steffan Gwyn, Jacob Harding, Mathilda Hardstone, Eden James, Megan Jenkins, Helen Lloyd, Alex Penfold, Ben Penfold, Holly Phillips, Kieran Roberts, Daniel Vernon.

Directed by Tim Baker

Designed by Max Jones

Composer and Musical Director – Dyfan Jones

Lighting Designed by Tina MacHugh

Dialect Coach – Sally Hague

Choreographer – Rachel Catherall

Fight Director – Kevin McCurdy

Sound Designer – Matthew Williams

Author's note on casting and production

This adaptation is designed to be played by a minimum cast of 16, doubling the minor parts. Of course it can be done with more, but the small ensemble feel is integral to the style of production, telling the story of hundreds and thousands of people.

The 2006 Clwyd Theatr Cymru production was cast as follows:

Man 1	Tom Joad
Man 2	Pa
Man 3	Al
Man 4	Connie (and other parts as indicated)
Man 5	Granpa (and other parts as indicated)
Man 6	Uncle John
Man 7	Casy
Man 8	Floyd (and other parts as indicated)
Man 9	Tractor Driver (and other parts as indicated)
Man 10	Ragged Man (and other parts as indicated)
Woman 1	Ma
Woman 2	Rose of Sharon
Woman 3	Grandma (and other parts as indicated)
Woman 4	Cafe Owner (and other parts as indicated)
Woman 5	Ensemble (other parts as appropriate)
Woman 6	Ensemble (other parts as appropriate)

Parts played are clearly marked in the text, and take into account practical considerations, for example leaving enough stage time for the actor playing Granpa to change after Granpa's death to reappear as Man 5.

In the 2006 production there were also nine children – Winfield and Ruthie, and seven others for the camp and crowd scenes. Crucial to the whole texture of the piece is music of the period, so the skills of banjo, harmonica, guitar and fiddle should be borne in mind when casting Men 8, 9, 10 and Women 4, 5 and 6.

Crucial to the style of the production – and to the world being created, is the way in which the family 'travel' and 'arrive' at the various locations on their journey. The set should be dominated by the truck as the key feature, which should be as realistic as possible. However, no attempt should be made to 'travel' as in wheels turning. Instead, the truck should be openly and obviously repositioned to represent the different locations and camps and other items brought on as appropriate. In the 2006 production this was achieved very effectively with a set consisting of a huge sky backdrop with little else but the truck. The centre section of the stage was a revolve in order to turn and reposition the truck. For the final scenes, two realistic boxcars were brought on stage. Locations were framed by sliding black flats opening and closing the playing space.

ACT ONE

Prologue

Music. MA *stands alone on the stage.*

MA We was in the truck, just setting off, leavin' the lan', when my boy Al said to me: "Ma, you scared a goin'? You scared a goin' to a new place?" I said, "A little, only it ain't like scared so much. I'm jus' a-waitin'. When somepin happens that I got to do somepin I'll do it." He said, "Ain't you thinkin' what's it gonna be like when we get there? Ain't you scared it won't be nice like we thought?" "No," I said quickly. "No, I ain't." You can't do that. I can't do that. It's too much livin' too many lives. Up ahead they's a thousan' lives we might live, but when it comes, it'll only be one. If I go ahead on all of 'em, it's too much. It's jus' the road goin' by for me. An' it's jus' how soon the family's gonna wanta eat. That's all I can do. I can't do no more. The family'd get upset if I done any more'n that. They all depen' on me jus' thinkin' about that.

(*The rest of the family are revealed.*)

We're the Joad family. We're Joads. We don't look up to nobody. Grampa's Grampa, he fought in the Revolution. We was farm people till the debt. And then – them other people come and they done somethin' to us. Ever' time they come seemed like they was whippin' me – all of us. They done something to me – made me feel mean. Made me feel ashamed. I jus' want to feel like people again.

(*The roar of a tractor fills the space. The engine dies, and the driver* (MAN 9) *appears through the dust cloud. He lifts his goggles and peers out.*)

TRACTOR DRIVER	You there! (*The rest of the company join the Joads, facing the* TRACTOR DRIVER. *It is hot and dusty.*) You better get out soon. I'm going through this dooryard after dinner. Got to keep the line straight. So I'm going through the dooryard. I got orders wherever there's a family not moved out – if I have an accident – you know, get too close and cave the house in a little – well, I might get a couple of dollars extra. And my youngest kid never had no shoes yet. Got to keep the line straight.
MAN 10	Why, ain't you Joe Davis's boy!
TRACTOR DR.	Sure.
WOMAN 5	Well, what you doing this kind of work for – against your own people?
TRACTOR DR.	I get three dollars a day. I got a wife and kids, we got to eat. Three dollars a day, and it comes every day.
MAN 6	But for your three dollars a day fifteen or twenty families can't eat at all.
WOMAN 6	Nearly a hundred people a day have to go out and wander on the roads for your three dollars. Is that right?
TRACTOR DR.	Can't think of that. Got to think of my own kids. Three dollars a day, and it comes every day. Times are changing, don't you know? Can't make a living on the land unless you've got two, five, ten thousand acres and a tractor. Crop land isn't for little guys like you any more. You try to get three dollars a day someplace. That's the only way. Get your three dollars a day, feed your kids. You got no call to worry about anybody's kids but your own. Git out of my way.
WOMAN 2	Where will we go?

TRACTOR DR.	Not for me to say. I'm going through this dooryard after dinner. Got to keep the line straight.
MAN 8	But we built it with our hands.
MAN 3	Straightened old nails to put the sheathing on.
GRANPA	We wired the rafters to the stringers with bailing wire.
PA	It's ours. We built it.
MAN 10	You bump it down – I'll be in the window with a rifle.
GRANPA	You even come too close and I'll pot you like a rabbit.
TRACTOR DR.	It's not me. There's nothing I can do. I'll lose my job if I don't do it. And look – suppose you kill me? They'll just hang you, but long before you're hung there'll be another guy on the tractor, and he'll bump the house down. You're not killing the right guy.
MAN 8	Who can we shoot? We don't aim to starve to death before we kill the man that's starving us.
TRACTOR DR.	I don't know. Maybe there's nobody to shoot. Maybe the thing isn't men at all. Maybe, the property's doing it. Anyway I told you my orders. Got to keep the line straight.

(*He goes. With a roar the tractor fires up again. As the company leave the stage they sing:*)

Oh sisters let's go down,
Let's go down, come on down,
Come on sisters let's go down,
Down in the river to pray.

Scene 1

CASY is squatting, looking out. A wide open space. In the distance, the collapsed farmhouse.

CASY
Yes, sir, that's my Saviour,
Jesus is my Saviour,
Jesus is my Saviour now.
On the level,
'S not the devil,
Jesus is my Saviour now.

(TOM JOAD *appears.*)

TOM
What happened here?

CASY
Now ain't you young Tom Joad, ol' Tom's boy? You wouldn' remember me, I guess.

TOM
Why, you're the preacher.

CASY
I was a preacher, Reverend Jim Casy was a Burning Busher. Used to howl out the name of Jesus to glory. And used to get an irrigation ditch so squirmin' full of repented sinners half of 'em like to drownded. But not no more. Just Jim Casy now. Ain't got the call no more. Got a lot of sinful ideas but they seem kinda sensible now.

TOM
What happened here? Where's my folks? Look at the house. All pushed outa shape. Somethin' knocked the hell outa her. Where's my folks?

CASY
Don't you know?

TOM
I ain't been home in four years.

CASY
Been out travelin' around?

TOM
Didn' you hear about me? I was in all the papers.

CASY
No, I never.

TOM	I killed a guy in a fight. We was drunk at a dance. He got a knife in me, an' I killed him with a shovel that was layin' there. Knocked his head plumb to squash. I got seven years, account of he had a knife in me. Got out in four – parole. (*He takes out a small bottle of whiskey, takes a drink.*) You ain't too damn holy to take a drink, are ya?
	(CASY *drinks.*)
CASY	Nice drinking liquor.
TOM	Aught to be, cost me a buck.
CASY	Yes sir. Then you ain't heard nothin' about your folks for four years?
TOM	Ain't heard nothin' about this. Where they gone?
CASY	Well, it's a funny thing, while back I was thinking I ain't seen your father ol' Tom in a bug's age, so thought I'd look in on him. Came an saw what you are seeing. Folks jus' kicked off the land. Met a fella jus' now, looking for rabbits and I asked him "What's the idea of kickin' the the folks off the lan?" An' he says, you know what kinda years we been havin'. Dust comin' up an' spoilin' ever'thing so a man didn't get enough crop to plug up an ant's ass. An' ever'body got bills at the grocery. Well, the folks that owns the lan' says, "We can't afford to keep no tenants". So they tractored all the tenants off a the lan'.
	(*A bearded, scraggy man runs on with a shotgun. He makes to hide, then recognises* TOM.)
CASY	Why here he is now –

MULEY	Well, I'll be damned, it's Tommy Joad. When'd you get out, Tommy?
TOM	Two days ago. Where's my folks, Muley?
MULEY	By God, it's lucky I come by and see you. Cause your Pa was worried. When they was fixin' to move I was settin' in the kitchen there. He says, "I'm worryin' myself about Tommy. S'pose he comes home an' they ain't nobody here. What'll he think?" I says. "I'll be aroun'". I says. "I'll be aroun' till hell freezes over. I'll keep my eye out for Tommy. There ain't nobody can run me out this country. An' they ain't done it, neither".
TOM	Where's my folks?
MULEY	Well, they was gonna stick her out when the bank come to tractorin' off the place. Your grampa stood out here with a rifle, an' he blowed the headlights off that tractor, but she come on just the same, an' bumped the hell outa the house, an' give her a shake like a dog shakes a rat. Well, it took somepin outa Tom. Kinda got into 'im. He ain't been the same ever since.
TOM	Muley, where's my folks?
MULEY	They're all at your Uncle John's.
TOM	Well, what they doin' there?
MULEY	Well, they been choppin' cotton, all of 'em, even the kids an' your grampa. Gettin' money together so they can shove on west. Gonna buy a car and shove on west where it's easy livin'. I tell ya, men, I'm stayin'. They ain't gettin' rid a me. I got a gun here. My pa come here fifty years ago. An' I ain't a-goin'.

(*We hear the sound of a motor car.*)

MULEY	Get down! That's the super'ntendent of this stretch a cotton.
TOM	We ain't doin' no harm. We ain't doin' nothin'.
MULEY	We're doin' somepin jus' bein' here.

(*The car passes. The men duck down.*)

	We're trespassin'. We can't stay. They been tryin' to catch me for two months. They's hundreds of families goin' out west, but I'm stayin'.
CASY	l gotta see them folks that's gone out on the road. I got a feelin' I got to see them. They gonna need help no preachin' can give 'em. They gonna need help. They got to live before they can afford to die.
TOM	You think you're comin' along, Casy?
CASY	Yeah, I'm goin' with you. An' when your folks start out on the road I'm goin' with them. An' where folks are on the road, I'm gonna be with them.
TOM	You're welcome, Ma always favored you. Said you was a preacher to trust. Think you'll come along, Muley?
MULEY	No. I'm stayin'. You think I'm touched? I ain't talked to nobody for a long time. I'm like a ol' graveyard ghos' goin' to neighbors' houses in the night. An' the houses all dark, standin' like miser'ble ratty boxes, but they was good parties an' dancin'. An' there was meetin's and shoutin' glory. They was weddin's, all in them houses. An' then I want to go in town an' kill folks. 'Cause what'd they take when they tractored the folks off the lan'? What'd they get so their 'margin a profit' was safe? What'd they get? God knows the lan' ain't no good.

Nobody been able to make a crop for years.
Place where folks live is them folks. They
ain't whole, out lonely on the road in a piled-
up car. They ain't alive no more. Them sons-a-
bitches killed them. I ain't talked to nobody
for a long time, I been sneakin' aroun' like a
ol' graveyard ghos'. You fellas think I'm
touched?

CASY No, you're lonely – but you ain't touched.

TOM Come on. You look after yourself, Muley.

(*They move off, leaving* MULEY.)

Scene 2

A garage lot in Oklahoma. SALESMEN. *They sing. Towards the end of the song the Joad jalopy is revealed.*

All you folks travellin' out west,
You gotta have wheels so get 'em from the best.
We've bargains a-plenty at the used car lot,
So come on down and see what we've got.
Come and get your used cars here.

Taken a little fancy to this Chevvy here.
She'll run forever – she'll get you there.
She's reliable, dependable, never been rolled.
Do a knock down price so consider it sold.
Come and spend your dollars here.

Ain't so easy tellin' salesman lies
To folks with nothing but hope in their eyes.
Break my heart sellin' stuff so rough,
But they's thousands goin', we can't get enough.
Come and get your used cars here.

We got Cadillacs, Buicks, Pontiacs and Fords
And Chevvies and Plymouths and Chandlers and more.
Good tyres, strong brakes, clutch fine, runs well,
Spin the patter to the punters and sell, sell, sell.

Fleece them ol' farmers for everything they've got.
Just move these jalopies off the lot!
Get 'em sold, get 'em shot, what you waitin' for?
Get a sale, close the deal, so we can sell more, more, more!

Hey all you folks movin' out west,
You gotta have wheels so get 'em from the best.

(*spoken*) And good luck all of you. Hope you make your fortune in California – oh you'll get there – in that. (*Pointing to the jalopy, by now revealed.*)

(*sung*) So thanks for your money and get on your way.
Come and get your used cars,
(You won't regret it),
Come and get your used cars . . . here!

Scene 3

Uncle John's *place. An old jalopy centre stage.* Pa *is working on the truck.* Tom *and* Casy *arrive.*

Tom	(*to* Casy) Holy Christ, they're fixin' to go! (*Calling to* Pa.) Hey Old Man!
Pa	What do you want? (*He sees* Tom.) It's Tommy. It's Tommy come home. Tommy, you ain't busted out?
Tom	Naw, I'm paroled. I'm free. I got my papers.
Pa	Tommy, we are goin' to California. But we was gonna write you a letter an' tell you. But you're back. You can go with us. You can go! Your Ma got a bad feelin' she ain't never gonna see you no more. She got that quiet look like when somebody died. Almost she don't want to go to California. Le's supprise her.

	Le's act like you never been away. Le's jus' see what your Ma says. (*He sees the preacher.*)
TOM	You remember the preacher, Pa? I met 'im on the road.
PA	Why sure. You're welcome, sir.
CASY	Glad to be here. It's a thing to see when a boy comes home.
PA	Tom. How'll we do her?
TOM	Don't le's scare her none.
PA	(*calling to* MA) Ma, there's a coupla fellas jus' come along the road, an' they wonder if we could spare a bite.
MA	(*from offstage / inside*) Let 'em come, We got a-plenty. Tell 'em they got to wash their han's.
PA	You wash your hands.
MA	Jus' lucky I made plenty bread this morning. (*She comes out and sees* TOM. *She rushes to him.*) Thank God, oh, thank God! (*And suddenly her face is worried.*) Tommy, you ain't wanted? You didn' bust loose?
TOM	No, Ma. Parole. I got the papers here.
MA	Well! We come mighty near to goin' without ya. An' we was wonderin' how in the worl' you could ever find us.
PA	Fooled ya, huh, Ma! We aimed to fool ya, and we done it. Jus' stood there like a hammered sheep. Wisht Grampa'd been here to see.
TOM	Where is Grampa? I ain't seen the ol' devil.
MA	Oh, him an' Gramna sleeps in the barn. Pa, run on out an' tell 'em Tommy's home.

PA	A course, I should of did it before. (*He runs off.* CASY *wanders away.*)
MA	Tommy.
TOM	Yeah?
MA	Tommy, I got to ask you. You ain't mad?
TOM	Mad, Ma?
MA	You ain't poisoned mad? You don't hate nobody? They didn' do nothin' in that jail to rot you out with crazy mad?
TOM	No, I was for a little while. But I ain't proud like some fellas. I let stuff run off'n me. All the time in stir I kep' away from stuff. I ain' mad, Ma – not in jail.
MA	Thank God!
TOM	But Ma, when I seen what they done to our house –
MA	Tommy, don't you go fightin 'em alone. They'll hunt you down like a coyote. They say there's a hun'erd thousand of us shoved out. Gettin' mad alone won't work. It's maybe we all need to get mad together .
TOM	Ma, you never was like this before!
MA	I never had my house pushed over, I never had my fambly stuck out on the road. I jus' hope things is all right in California. Ever'one saying how nice it's gonna be an' how much work they is, an' high wages an' all. Your father got a han'bill on orange paper, tellin' how they need folks to work . . . I'm scared of stuff so nice. Is it too nice, Tommy? Is there too much faith, Tommy?

TOM	"Don't roust your faith bird-high an' you won't do no crawlin' with the worms".
MA	I know that's right. That's Scripture, ain't it?
TOM	Look, Ma, stop your worryin'. I'm a-gonna tell you somepin about bein' in the pen. You can't go thinkin' when you're gonna be out. You'd go nuts. You got to think about that day, an' then the nex' day, about the ball game Saturday. That's what you got to do. Ol' timers does that. A new young fella gets buttin' his head on the cell door. He's thinkin' how long it's gonna be. Whyn't you do that? Jus' take ever' day.
MA	That's a good way. Yes, that's a good way.
TOM	Besides, I'm coming with you. I'm with you all the way.
MA	Tommy!
	(*She hugs him.* GRANPA *enters with* GRANMA.)
GRANPA	Praise Gawd fur vittory! Praise Gawd fur vittory!
GRANMA	Praise Gawd fur vittory!
GRANPA	Look at him, a jailbird. Ain't been no Joads in jail for a hell of a time. Got no right to put 'im in jail. Sonsabitches! He done just what I'd do. How are ya, Tommy?
TOM	Okay. How ya keepin' yaself?
GRANPA	Full a piss an' vinegar. Jus, like I said, they ain't a-gonna keep no Joad in jail. I says, "Tommy'll come a-bustin' outa that jail like a bull through a corral fence". An' you done it. Now get outa my way, I'm hungry.
TOM	Ain't he a heller?

GRANMA	A wicketer man never lived. He's goin' to hell on a poker, praise Gawd!
TOM	Good to see you, Granma –
MA	We ain't got room to set down. Jus' get yaself a plate an' set down wherever ya can.
TOM	Hey! Where's the preacher? He was right here. Where'd he go?
GRANMA	Preacher? You got a preacher? Go git him. We'll have a grace. Go git the preacher.
TOM	Hey, Jim! Jim Casy! Oh, Casy! (CASY *emerges.*) What was you doin', hidin'?
CASY	Well, no. But a fella shouldn' butt his head in where a fambly got fambly stuff. I was jus' settin' a-thinkin'.
TOM	Come on in an' eat, Granma wants a grace.
CASY	But I ain't a preacher no more.
GRANPA	Preacher? We got a preacher? Oh him? Oh, he's all right. I always liked him since I seen him ruttin' in a field with – (*. . . that redhead girl . . .*)
GRANMA	Shut up, you sinful ol' goat.
TOM	Aw, come on. Give her a grace. Don't do you no harm, an' she likes 'em.
CASY	I got to tell you, I ain't a preacher no more. But if me jus' bein' glad to be here an' bein' thankful for people that's kind and generous, if that's enough why, I'll say that kinda grace.
GRANMA	Say her an' get in a word about us goin' to California.
CASY	Well – I been thinkin'. I been in the hills, thinkin', almost you might say like Jesus went

into the wilderness to think His way out of a mess of troubles. Only He couldn't figure nothin' out. Well there was the hills, an' there was me, an' we wasn't separate no more. We was one thing. An' that one thing was holy. An' as I got thinkin', only it wasn't thinkin', it was deeper down than thinkin'. I got thinkin' how we was holy when we was one thing, an' mankin' was holy when it was one thing. An' it only got unholy when one mis'able little fella got the bit in his teeth an' run off his own way, kickin' an' draggin' an' fightin'. Fella like that bust the holiness. But when they're all workin' together, not one fella for another fella, but one fella kind of harnessed to the whole shebang – that's right, that's holy. An' then I got thinkin' I don't even know what I mean by holy. I can't say no grace like I use' ta say. I'm glad of the holiness of food. I'm glad there's love here. That's all. Amen.

ALL Amen. (*They eat.*)

TOM So you bought a truck?

PA Your brother Al looked her over before we bought her. He says she's all right.

TOM Where's he now?

PA Well, he's a billygoatin' aroun' the country. He don't think of nothin' but girls and engines. Ain't been in nights for a week.

GRANPA I was worse, I was much worse. When I was a young fella. He's just a squirt, an' punkinsoft. But I ain't nowheres near the fella I was. Got to take a piss –

MA You make sure you button up down there! They don' let people run aroun' with their clothes unbutton' in California!

GRANPA	They don't? Well, I'll show 'em! They think they're going to show me how to act out there? Why I'll go roun' a-hangin' out all day long if I want to!
TOM	Where's Uncle John? Where's my sister Rosasharn? Where's lil' Ruthie an' Winfield?
PA	Your Uncle John took 'em all to Sallisaw with a load a stuff to sell: pump, tools, chickens, an' all the stuff we brung over. An' if I ain't mistaken, there's a young smart aleck draggin' his tail home right now. Looks purty wore out, too.

(AL *enters.*)

TOM	Hello, Al.
PA	He's just like a tom-cat. Smart aleck young buck, an' his nuts is just a-eggin' him on.
TOM	Jesus, you're growin' like a bean! I wouldn't of knowed you.
AL	Did – did you bust out? Of jail?
TOM	No I got paroled.
AL	Oh. (*A little disappointed. He draws* TOM *to one side.*) You comin' with us? You going over the state line? They catch you, they send you back to do the rest of your time.

(TOM *motions to him to shut his mouth as* UNCLE JOHN, ROSE OF SHARON, CONNIE, RUTHIE *and* WINFIELD *enter.*)

UNCLE JOHN	Why, it's Tom! Tom's back!
THE KIDS	Where is he? Where's Tom?
TOM	Hello, how you kids doin'?

THE KIDS	All right.
	(*"They stood apart and watched him secretly, the great brother who had killed a man and been in prison."*)
TOM	How are you, Uncle John? Why, it's Rosasharn.
ROSE OF SHARON	Tom. This is Connie, my husband.
	(CONNIE *steps forward.*)
PA	By God! You don't even know Rosasharn's married to Connie Rivers. You 'member Connie. Nice young fella. An' Rosasharn's 'bout four five months now.
TOM	Well, I see you been busy.
ROSE OF SHAR.	You do not see, not yet.
TOM	(*eying* CONNIE *with suspicion*) When's it gonna be?
ROSE OF SHAR.	Oh, not for a long time!
CONNIE	Not till nex' winter.
TOM	Gonna get 'im bore in a orange ranch, huh? In one a them white houses with orange trees all aroun'?
ROSE OF SHAR.	Yep!
	(*All laugh.*)
MA	Tommy's home! And we're all going to California!
UNCLE JOHN	(*breaking the moment*) Eighteen dollars. For every movable thing we had. The horses, the wagon, the implements, and all the furniture from the house. Eighteen dollars. We argued

and then he had told us he didn't want the stuff
at any price. So we had to take his offer.

(*A downbeat.*)

PA
So we got total of hunderd fifty-four dollars to
get to California.

AL
We gonna need better tires. These here won't
last. She's old but I gave her a good goin'-
over. Didn' listen to the fella tellin' me what a
hell of a bargain she was. Stuck my finger in
the differential and they wasn't no sawdust. I
opened the gear box an' they wasn't no
sawdust. Test' her clutch an' rolled her wheels
for line. Went under her an' her frame ain't
splayed none. She never been rolled.

GRANPA
You're all right, Al – I was a squirt jus'like
you, a-fartin' aroun' like a dog-wolf. But when
they was a job, I done it. You've growed up
good.

TOM
I'd like to say – well, the preacher – he wants
to go along. We've knowed him a long time.
Talks a little wild sometimes, but he talks
sensible.

PA
Well – kin we feed a extra mouth? Kin we, Ma?

MA
Why, we'll do what we will. You're welcome,
Sir.

PA
Wait, s'pose there just ain't room? S'pose we
jus' can't all get in the truck?

MA
There ain't room now, there ain't room for
more'n six, an' look at all of us. One more
ain't gonna hurt; an' a man, strong an' healthy,
ain't never no burden.

AL
When do you think we should go, Pa?

PA   Early in the morning, we'll get the truck loaded, all but the beds, an' nex' morning off we'll go.

AL   Hardly is a day's work in all that.

TOM   We'll be moonin' aroun' all day, lookin' for somepin to do. We could get ready by daylight an' go.

UNCLE JOHN   What we hangin' aroun' for? I want to get shut of this. Now we're goin', why don't we go?

              (*They all begin to move forward, as it were looking down the road.*)

AL   Whyn't we go now?

MA   Get sleep on the way –

PA   They say it's two thousan' miles. That's a hell of a long ways.

TOM   What are we waitin' for?

              (*Music. They pack the last items on the jalopy. Very upbeat.*)

AL   You glad to be goin', Pa?

PA   Huh? Well – sure. Leastwise – yeah. We had hard times here. 'Course it'll be all different out there – plenty work, an' ever'thing nice an' green, an' little white houses an' oranges growin' aroun'.

ROSE OF SHAR. Is it all oranges everwhere?

PA   Well, maybe not everwhere, but plenty places.

ROSE OF SHAR. (*to* CONNNIE) It's all oranges everwhere.

AL   Holy Jesus, them springs is flat as hell. Lucky I blocked under 'em.

(They pile into the truck, the music hovers as they are about to 'move off'.)

GRANMA   I like to think how nice it's gonna be, in California. Never cold.

ROSE OF SHAR.   An' fruit ever' place, an' people just bein' in the nicest places, little white houses in among the orange trees.

PA   If we all get jobs an' all work –

UNCLE JOHN   Maybe we can get one of them little white houses!

AL   An' the little fellas go out an' pick oranges right off the tree.

GRANMA   They ain't gonna be able to stand it, they'll get to yellin' so.

GRANPA   They's oranges an', by God, they's grapes out there, just a-hangin' over inta the road. Know what I'm a-gonna do? I'm gonna pick me a wash tub full a grapes, an' I'm gonna set in 'em, an' scrooge aroun', an' let the juice run down my pants!!

(Laughter, and they settle as if the truck is 'moving off'. Music lifts and rises, representing 'travelling'.)

Scene 4

Music drives on under this sequence. The rest of the company crowd around the truck, as a "chorus". Where possible, in all these sequences, the company are accompanying themselves with music.

WOMAN 4   Highway 66 is the road to California.
AL   Listen to the motor.
MAN 8   Listen to the wheels.

UNCLE JOHN	Listen with your ears and with your hands on the steering wheel;
MAN 10	Listen with the palm of your hand on the gear-shift lever;
WOMAN 6	Listen with your feet on the floor boards.
ALL	Listen!
GRANPA	'F we can on'y get to California where the oranges grow before this here ol' jug blows up.
ROSE OF SHAR.	'F we on'y can!
PA	How far's the next town?
MAN 9	I seen forty-two cars a you fellas go by yesterday.
MAN 10	Where you all come from?
WOMAN 4/ MAN 8	Where you all goin'?
ALL	California!
WOMAN 4	Well, California's a big State.
MAN 10	It ain't that big. The whole United States ain't that big.
MAN 8	It ain't big enough. There ain't room enough for you an' me,
MAN 9	For your kind an' my kind,
WOMAN 6	For rich and poor together all in one country,
MAN 10	For thieves and honest men.
WOMAN 6	Whyn't you go back where you come from?
TOM	This is a free country. Fella can go where he wants.
MAN 9	That's what you think! Ever hear of the border patrol on the California line?
WOMAN 6	If you can't buy no real estate they don't want you!
TOM	It's a free country.
WOMAN 5	You're jus' as free as you got jack to pay for it.
PA	In California they got high wages. I got a han'bill here tells about it.

Woman 4	So've we.
Man 8	We all got handbills.
Woman 4	I seen folks comin' back.
Man 8	Somebody's kiddin' you!
Woman 5	Two hundred and fifty thousand people over the road.
Woman 6	Fifty thousand old cars – wounded, steaming.
Woman 4	Where does the courage come from?
Man 9	Where does the terrible faith come from?
Woman 5	The people in flight from the terror behind – strange things happen to them, some so bitterly cruel and some so beautiful that their faith is rekindled forever.
	(*During this sequence a campsite is constructed around the truck, which at the very end is re-positioned so that it has 'arrived'.*)

Scene 5

Tom	(*to a man passing by, with a child*) Any law 'gainst folks stoppin' here for the night?
Man 10	I dunno, We on'y stopped here 'cause we couldn' git no further.
Tom	Any water here?
Child	They's water up there beyond they'll let ya take a bucket of.
Tom	Well, ya 'spose we could camp down 'longside?
Man 10	We don't own it, we only stopped here 'cause our goddamn ol' trap wouldn' go no further. Proud to have ya.
Tom	Much obliged.

(He signals to the family. Slowly they climb down. MA gathers the kids around her.)

MA
Now you go git water right down there. Ask nice. Say, "Please, kin we git a bucket a water?" and say, "Thank you". An' carry it back together helpin', an' don't spill none. An' if you see stick wood to burn bring it on.

KIDS
Right –

(They scamper off. CONNIE helps ROSE OF SHARON down.)

ROSE OF SHAR.
We seed a lot of fine cars on the highway, Connie. How'd you like to be goin' along in one of them?

CONNIE
Maybe after. If they's plenty work in California, we'll git our own car. But them, them kind costs as much as a good size house. I rather have the house.

ROSE OF SHAR.
I like to have the house an' one a them, but 'course the house would be first because –

(She indicates her belly.)

CONNIE
You feel awright?

ROSE OF SHAR.
Tard, jus' tar'd ridin' in the sun.

CONNIE
We got to do that or we won't never get to California.

ROSE OF SHAR.
I know.

(GRANPA staggers out of the truck.)

AL
You sick, Grampa? Ma!

GRANPA
You goddamn right, sicker'n hell.

MA	Get a blanket and lay Granpa down. That's right. Come on now, You'll git some rest.

(*Without warning* GRAMPA *begins to cry.* MA *rushes over to him and puts her arms around him. She lifts him to his feet, her broad back straining. A mattress is quickly fetched from the truck and laid on the ground.* MA *half lifts, half helps him onto the mattress.*)

MA	He must be good an' sick. He ain't never done that before. Never seen him blubberin' in my life. (*To* CASY.) You been aroun' sick people, Grampa's sick. Won't you go take a look at him? (GRAMPA *is wheezing and groaning.*)
CASY	Feeling kinda tired, Grampa?
UNCLE JOHN	Know what's wrong?
CASY	Do you?
UNCLE JOHN	I think so.
CASY	What?
UNCLE JOHN	Might be wrong. I wouldn' like to say.
CASY	Would you say maybe he's workin' up a stroke?
UNCLE JOHN	I'd say that. I seen it three times before.
GRANMA	What's goin' on?
MA	Granma wants to come over. Would she better?
CASY	Well I don't know . . .
MA	(*she moves over to* GRANMA) He's awright, Granma. He's jus' takin' a little res'.

GRANMA	Well, I want ta see him. He's a tricky devil. He wouldn't never let ya know. (*She comes over.*) What's the matter 'th you? (*She kicks him.*) He's sulkin' – I tol' you he was tricky. He didn't really want to come. He was gonna sneak away this mornin' so he wouldn't have to come. An' then his hip got a hurtin'. He's jus' sulkin'. I seen him when he wouldn' talk to nobody before.
CASY	He ain't sulkin', Granma! He's sick!
GRANMA	Sick bad, you think?
CASY	Purty bad, Granma.
GRANMA	Well, why ain't you prayin'? You're a preacher, ain't you?
CASY	I tol' you, Granma. I ain't a preacher no more.
GRANMA	Pray anyway, you know all the stuff by heart!
CASY	I can't, I don't know what to pray for or who to pray to!
GRANMA	He won't pray!

(GRAMPA *cries out and struggles.*)

UNCLE JOHN	His tongue, his tongue! His tongue!

(CASY *struggles with the dying old man.*)

GRANMA	Pray! Pray, you! Pray, I tell ya! Pray, goddamn you!
CASY	Our Father who art in Heaven, hallowed be Thy name –
GRANMA	Glory!
CASY	Thy kingdom come, Thy will be done on earth as it is in Heaven –

GRANMA	Amen.
	(*A long gasping sigh comes from the open mouth, and then a crying release of air.*)
CASY	Give us this day our daily bread and forgive us – (GRANPA *is dead.*)
GRANMA	Hallelujah! Go on!
CASY	Amen.
PA	What was it?
CASY	Stroke. A good quick stroke.
	(*The family gathers round.*)
PA	We got to figger what to do. They's laws. You got to report a death, an' when you do that, they either take forty dollars for the undertaker or they take him for a pauper. We only got eighty seven dollars left.
UNCLE JOHN	We never did have no paupers.
TOM	Maybe we got to learn. We never got booted off no land before, neither.
PA	We never took nothin' we couldn' pay; we never suffered no man's charity. Grampa buried his pa with his own hand, done it in dignity, an' shaped the grave nice with his own shovel.
UNCLE JOHN	The law says different now.
PA	Sometimes the law can't be foller'd no way. Not with dignity, anyways. They's lots a times you can't. Sometimes a fella got to sift the law. I'm sayin' now I got the right to bury my own pa. Anybody got somepin to say?
CASY	Law changes, but "got to's" go on. You got the right to do what you got to do.

PA	It's your right too, John. You got any word against?
UNCLE JOHN	No word against.
PA	We got to get to California 'fore our money gives out.
TOM	Sometimes fellas workin' dig up a man an' then they raise hell an' figger he been killed. The gov'ment's got more interest in a dead man than a live one. I offer we put a note of writin' in a bottle an' lay it with Grampa, tellin' who he is an' how he died, an' why he's buried here.
PA	Tha's good. Wrote out in a nice han'. Be not so lonesome too, knowin' his name is there with 'im, not jus' a old fella lonesome underground. Any more stuff to say?
PA	(*to* MA) You'll lay him out?
MA	I'll lay 'im out. Gimme two half dollars.
	(PA *gives her the dollars. She lays the old man out.*)
AL	Granma took it good.
PA	Why, she's so old, maybe she don't even rightly know what happened. Maybe she won't really know for quite a while. Besides, us folks takes a pride holdin' in. That's what Grampa used to say. Anybody can break down. It takes a man not to. We always try to hold in.
AL	Least we got a preacher to see him in, an' his folks is all aroun'.
ROSE OF SHAR.	(*to* CONNIE) Do you think it will hurt the baby?
CONNIE	How d'ya mean?

ROSE OF SHAR. I heard a sayin', a chile born outa sorrow'll be a happy chile, isn't that so?

CONNIE I heard it like that too. An' I heard the other: born outa too much joy'll be a doleful boy.

ROSE OF SHAR. I'm all jumpy inside.

CONNIE You look after yourself.

(*The rest of the company, who have been as other travellers in the background, join. A hymn, as* GRANPA *is laid out and buried. During an underscore section,* TOM *reads the passage he has written, then puts it in a bottle.*)

(*sung*) My heavenly home is bright and fair,
I feel like travelling on.
No pain and death can enter there,
I feel like travelling on.

Yes I feel like travelling on,
I feel like travelling on.
My heavenly home is bright and fair,
I feel like travelling on.

(*Underscore continues under speech.*)

TOM This here is William James Joad, dyed of a stroke, old, old man. His fokes bured him becaws they got no money to pay for funerls. Nobody kilt him. Jus' a stroke an he dyed. "Blessed is he whose transgression is forgiven, whose sin is covered".

(PA *turns to* CASY.)

PA Won't you say a few words? Ain't none of our folks ever been buried without a few words.

CASY I'll say 'em, it'll be a short one. This here ol' man jus' lived a life an' jus' died out of it. I don't know whether he was good or bad, but that don't matter much. He was alive, an' that's what matters. An' now he's dead, an' that don't matter. Heard a fella tell a poem one time, an' he says "all that lives is holy". Got to thinkin', an' purty soon it means more than the words says. An' I wouldn't pray for a ol' fella that's dead. He's awright. He got a job to do, but it's all laid out for 'im an' there's only one way to do it. But us, we got a job to do, an' they's a thousan' ways, an' we don' know which one to take. An' if I was to pray, it'd be for the folks that don' know which way to turn. Grampa here, he got the easy straight. Amen.

ALL   Amen.

MA   Rosasharn, like a good girl go lay down with Granma. She needs somebody now.

AL   Funny thing is losin' Grampa ain't made me feel no different than I done before. I ain't no sadder than I was.

CASY   It's just the same thing as leavin' your home. Grampa an' the old place, they was jus' the same thing.

AL   It's a goddamn shame. He been talkin' what he's gonna do, how he gonna squeeze grapes over his head an' let the juice run in his whiskers, an' all stuff like that.

CASY   He was foolin', all the time. I think he knowed it.

(*They slowly pack the truck.*)

Scene 6

Six of the company come forward, address the audience, as music plays.

WOMAN 6   The Western States became nervous under the beginning change. Texas and Oklahoma,

	Kansas and Arkansas, New Mexico, Arizona, California.
MAN 10	And amongst the straining jalopies on their way to California, there are big cars on the highway too.
WOMAN 4	In them, little pot-bellied men in light suits and panama hats; clean, pink men with puzzled, worried eyes, with restless eyes.
WOMAN 5	Worried men who reassure themselves that business is noble and not the curious ritualized thievery they know it is; that business men are intelligent in spite of the records of their stupidity; that they are kind and charitable in spite of the principles of sound business; that their lives are rich instead of the thin tiresome routines they know; and that a time is coming when they will not be afraid any more.
MAN 9	In Al and Suzi's diner, off the highway, two truck drivers, our people, sip Java and eat banana cream pie.
WOMAN 6	An old 6 Nash sedan pulls wearily off the highway. The back seat piled nearly to the ceiling with sacks, with pots and pans, and on the very top, right up against the ceiling, two boys ride. A dark-haired, hatchet-faced man gets slowly out. And the two boys slide down from the load and hit the ground.

(MAN 8 *becomes the* HUNGRY MAN, WOMAN 4 *plays* SUZI. *The next sequence is played very minimally.*)

HUNGRY MAN	Can we git some water, ma'am?
SUZI	Sure, go ahead.
HUNGRY MAN	Could you see your way to sell us a loaf of bread, ma'am? We need bread and there ain't nothin' for quite a piece, they say.

Suzi	If we sell bread we gonna run out.
Hungry Man	We're hungry.
Suzi	Whyn't you buy a san'widge? We got nice san'widges, hamburgs.
Hungry Man	We'd sure admire to do that, ma'am. But we can't. We got to make a dime do all of us. We ain't got but a little.
Suzi	We only got fifteen-cent loafs. This here is a fifteen-cent loaf.
Hungry Man	Won't you – can't you see your way to cut off ten cents' worth?
Suzi	Can't do that.
Woman 5	Al looks through from the kitchen.
Man 10 as Al	Goddamn it, Suzi. Give 'em the loaf!
Hungry Man	No, we want ta buy ten cents'worth of it. We got it figgered awful close, mister, to get to California.
Suzi	You can have it, the whole loaf, for ten cents.
Hungry Man	That'd be robbin' you, ma'am.
Suzi	Go ahead! Take it!
Hungry Man	Thank you ma'am. May soun' funny to be so tight. We got a thousan' miles to go, an' we don' know if we'll make it. Come on boys. (*He pauses.*) Is them penny candy ma'am?
Suzi	Which ones?
Woman 5	The truck drivers look up, listening. The two little boys are like statues. Al listens from the kitchen.

HUNGRY MAN	There, them stripy ones.
WOMAN 6	The little boys raise their eyes to her face and they stop breathing.
SUZI	Oh them. Well, no – them's two for a penny.
HUNGRY MAN	Oh. Well, gimme two then, ma'am.
WOMAN 5	The boys expel their held breath softly.
HUNGRY MAN	Thank you, ma'am.
WOMAN 6	And they go. The truck drivers have watched it all.
MAN 9 AS DRIVER 1	Them wasn't two-for-a-penny candy.
SUZI	What's that to you?
DRIVER 1	Them was nickel apiece candy.
SUZI	What's that to you, boys?
MAN 10 AS DRIVER 2	We got to get goin'. We're droppin' time.
WOMAN 5	They reach in their pockets. One puts a coin on the counter and the other follows.
DRIVER 1	So long.
WOMAN 6	And the door slams.
SUZI	Hey! Wait a minute. You got change.
DRIVER 1	You go to hell Suzi.
SUZI	I'll see you tomorrow Mac.
WOMAN 5	This is the movement the great owners fear; this is the movement from the 'I' to the 'we' – the potential of unity.

WOMAN 4   This is the thing to bomb.

(*The music rises to a crescendo, then subsides as the truck 'arrives'.*)

Scene 7

The truck has "stopped". A few of the family clamber out wearily. Another makeshift camp.

PA   (*returning from looking around*) Got shade an' got water in pipes.

MA   (*to* KIDS) Go and get some water.

PA   How is everyone?

MA   Seems like Granma ain't got no sense no more. Like a little baby. Don' speak to nobody, don' seem to reco'nize nobody, jus' talks on like she's talkin' to Grampa.

(*The* PROPRIETOR (MAN 9) *comes over. A scowling, ungracious man.*)

PROPRIETOR   You folks wanta camp here? If you wanta camp I here it'll cost you two bits. Get a place to camp an' water an' wood. An' nobody won't bother you. Welcome to New Mexico.

TOM   What the hell. We can sleep in the ditch right beside the road, an' it won't cost nothin'.

PROPRIETOR   Deputy sheriff comes on by in the night. Might make it tough for ya. Got a law against sleepin' out in this State. Got a law about vagrants.

TOM   If we pay you a half a dollar we ain't vagrants, huh?

PROPRIETOR   That's right.

TOM	Deputy sheriff ain't your brother'n law by any chance? (*The family laugh.*)
PROPRIETOR	No, he ain't. An' the time ain't come yet when us local folks got to take no talk from you goddamn bums, neither.
TOM	It don't trouble you none to take our two bits. An' when'd we get to be bums? We ain't asked ya for nothin'. All of us bums, huh? Well, we ain't askin' no nickels from you for the chance to lay down an' rest.
PA	Come off it, Tom.
TOM	Sure, I'll come off it. I don't wanta make no trouble. It's a hard thing to be named a bum. I ain't afraid I'll go for you an' your deputy with my mitts here now, or jump Jesus. But there ain't no good in it.
PROPRIETOR	We all got to make a livin'.
TOM	Yeah, on'y I wisht they was some way to make her 'thout takin' her away from somebody else.
PA	Tom. Leave be. What do you think, Ma? We only got fifty dollars left.
MA	Ever'body's so goddamn tired an' wore out an' mis'able, let's stay here. We got to 'cause Granma's so tired an' wore out.
PA	She any better now?
MA	Well, she's a-sleepin'
PA	(*offering money*) Here.
PROPRIETOR	Camp where you like.

PA	Al, Tom, John, Connie – let's take a look around.
MA	I'll see to Granma and Rosharn. (*She calls for* ROSE OF SHARON.) Come help me with Granma.
ROSE OF SHAR.	Ma, Ma, when we get there, all you gonna pick fruit an' kinda live in the country, ain't you?
MA	We ain't there yet, We don't know what it's like. We got to see.
ROSE OF SHAR.	Me an' Connie don't want to live in the country no more, We got it all planned up what we gonna do.
MA	Ain't you gonna stay with us – with the family?
ROSE OF SHAR.	Well, we talked all about it, me an' Connie. Ma, we wanna live in a town. Connie gonna get a job in a store or maybe a fact'ry. An' he's gonna study at home, maybe radio, so he can git to be a expert an' maybe later have his own store. An' we'll go to pitchers whenever. An' Connie says I'm gonna have a doctor when the baby's born; an' he says we'll see how times is, an' maybe I'll go to a hospiddle. An' we'll have a car, little car. An' after he studies at night, why it'll be nice, an' he tore a page outa Western Love Stories, an' he's gonna send off for a course, 'cause it don't cost nothin' to send off. Says right on that clipping. I seen it. An', why they even get you a job when you take that course radios, it is nice clean work, and a future. An' we'll live in town an' go to pitchers whenever, an' well, I'm gonna have a 'lectric iron, an' the baby'll have all new stuff. Connie says all new stuff white an' well, you seen in the catalogue all the stuff they got for a baby. Maybe right at first while Connie's studyin' at home it won't be so easy, but well, when the baby comes, maybe he'll be all done studyin' an' we'll have

	a place, little bit of a place. We don't want nothin' fancy, but we want it nice for the baby.

MA We don' want you to go 'way from us. It ain't good for folks to break up.

(PA, AL, JOHN, CASEY *and* TOM *are talking with a group of men – a* RAGGED MAN (MAN 10) *goes past.*)

PA Can't find nowhere as good as this. We'll camp here –

RAGGED MAN You folks all goin' out West?

AL Yeah.

RAGGED MAN You folks must have a nice little pot a money.

TOM No, we ain't got no money. But there's plenty of us to work, an' we're all good men.

AL Get good wages out there an' we'll put em together. We'll make out.

(*The* RAGGED MAN *stares and then he laughs, and his laughter turns to a high whinnying giggle.*)

RAGGED MAN You goin' out there oh, Christ! You goin' out an' get good wages oh, Christ! Pickin' oranges maybe? Gonna pick peaches?

PA We gonna take what they got. They got lots a stuff to work in –

TOM What's so goddamn funny about that?

RAGGED MAN You folks all goin' to California, I bet. Me I'm comin' back. I been there. I'm goin' back to starve. I rather starve all over at once.

PA What the hell you talkin' about? I got a han'bill says they got good wages, an' little while ago I seen a thing in the paper says they need folks to pick fruit.

RAGGED MAN Listen, I ain't gonna fret you mister –

PA Course you ain't gonna fret me. I got a han'bill says they need men. Don't make no sense if they don't need men. Costs money for them bills. They wouldn' put 'em out if they didn' need men.

RAGGED MAN I don' wanna fret you.

PA You done some jackassin'. You ain't gonna shut up now. My han'bill says they need men. You laugh an' say they don't. Now, which one's a liar?

RAGGED MAN Alright. Han'bill's right. They need men.

PA Then why the hell you stirrin' us up laughin'?

RAGGED MAN Cause you don't know what kind a men they need. Look. How many men they say they want on your han'bill?

PA Eight hunderd, an' that's in one little place.

RAGGED MAN Orange color han'bill?

PA Why yes.

RAGGED MAN Give the name a the fella says so and so, labor contractor?

(PA *reaches in his pocket and brings out the folded handbill.*)

PA That's right. Howd you know?

RAGGED MAN Look. This fella wants eight hundred men. So he prints up five thousand of them things an' maybe twenty thousan' people sees 'em. An' maybe two, three thousan' folks gets movin'

	account a this here han'bill. Folks that's crazy with worry.
PA	That don't make no sense!
RAGGED MAN	Not till you see the fella that put out this here bill. You'll see him, or somebody that's workin' for him. You'll be a campin' by a ditch, you an' fifty other famblies. An' he'll look in your tent an' see if you got anything lef' to eat. An' if you got nothin', he says, "Wanna job?" An' you'll say, "I sure do, mister. I'll sure thank you for a chance to do some work". An' he'll say, "I can use you". An' you'll say, "When do I start?" An' he'll tell you where to go, an' what time, an' then he'll go on. Maybe he needs two hunderd men, so he talks to five hunderd, an' they tell other folks, an' when you get to the place, they's a thousan' men. This here fella says, "I'm payin' twenty cents an hour."
PA	Twenty cents?
RAGGED MAN	An' maybe half a the men walk off. But they's still five hunderd that's so goddamn hungry they'll work for nothin' but biscuits. Well, this here fella's got a contract to pick them peaches or chop that cotton. You see now? The more fellas he can get, an' the hungrier, less he's gonna pay. An' he'll get a fella with kids if he can, 'cause – hell, I says I wasn't gonna fret ya. I says I wasn't gonna fret ya, an' here I'm a-doin' it. You gonna go on. You ain't goin back. Lemme tell ya what to do when ya meet that fella says he got work. Lemme tell ya. Ast him . . .

(*The* PROPRIETOR *has come over and is listening.*)

PROPRIETOR	You sure you ain't one of these here troublemakers? You sure you ain't a labor faker?

RAGGED MAN	I swear to God I ain't!
PROPRIETOR	They's plenty of 'em, goin' aroun' stirrin' up trouble. Gettin' folks mad. Chiselin' in. They's plenty of 'em. Time's gonna come when we string 'em all up, all them troublemakers. We gonna run 'em outa the country. Man wants to work, okay. If he don't, the hell with him. We ain't gonna let him stir up trouble.
RAGGED MAN	I tried to tell you folks. Somepin it took me a year to find out. Took two kids dead, took my wife dead to show me. But I can't tell you. I should of knew that. Nobody couldn't tell me, neither. I can't tell ya about them little fellas layin' in the tent with their bellies puffed out an' jus' skin on their bones, an' shiverin' an' whinin' like pups, an' me runnin' aroun' tryin' to get work not for money, not for wages!
	(*The* RAGGED MAN *goes.*)
AL	Well, gettin' late. Got to get to sleep.
PROPRIETOR	Probl'y shif'less. They's so goddamn many shif'less fellas on the road now. Well, time to close up anyways.
TOM	No more halfbucks rollin' down the road, I guess –
PROPRIETOR	Don't you go a-sassin' me. I 'member you. You're one of these here troublemakers.
TOM	Damn right, I'm bolshevisky.
PROPRIETOR	They's too damn many of you kinda guys aroun'.
	(PROPRIETOR *goes. The men walk over to the truck.*)
PA	S'pose he's tellin' the truth – that fella?

CASY	He's tellin' the truth, awright. The truth for him. He wasn't makin' nothin' up.
TOM	How about us? Is that the truth for us?
CASY	I don' know.
PA	I don' know.

(MA *comes out from the back of the truck.*)

MA	Granma finally dozed off. (*She senses the atmosphere.*) What's goin' on?
PA	Fella was jus' sayin' –
TOM	(*interrupting*) Funny what he says. Says they's lots a folks on the way.
PA	That's right. Ever'body here?
MA	Yep. Let's all get to sleep now.

(*They settle for the night. A beat.* GRANMA *screams from the truck.*)

GRANMA	Will! Will! You come here, Will. Tol' him to come right here, I'll catch him. I'll take the hair off 'n him!
ROSE OF SHAR.	(*coming out of the back of the truck*) She's awful sick.
GRANMA	Will! You're dirty! You ain't never gonna get clean. Wipe your feet, Will, you dirty pig!
MA	(*having hardly put her head down*) Maybe if we can get her where it ain't so hot, She's wore out with the road an' the heat. She's jus' wore out. Get a little res', an' she'll be well.

(ROSE OF SHARON *moves off. Sometime during the following* CONNIE *joins her.* TOM *is sleeping under the running board. Shadowy figures. A torch. We can just make out a* COP (MAN 8) *and the* PROPRIETOR.)

PROPRIETOR   More of these goddamn Okies. Wanna settle here.

COP   We'll give them one night. If they're still here tomorra, we'll run 'em in. These people sure have got nerve.

PROPRIETOR   What you mean?

COP   Well, crossin' in a jalopy like this. I'd hate to be doing it. Takes more nerve than I've got.

PROPRIETOR   It don't take no nerve to do somepin when there ain't nothin' else you can do.

COP   Jesus, I'd hate to start out in a jalopy like that. But then I got sense.

PROPRIETOR   These goddamn Okies got no sense and no feeling. They ain't human.

COP   A human being wouldn't live like they do.

PROPRIETOR   A human being couldn't stand it to be so dirty and miserable.

COP   They ain't a hell of a lot better than gorillas.

TOM   (*who can take no more*) You wanna say that again, mister? To my face? What you said 'bout my folks?

COP   Why look what just dropped down from a tree – it's a gorilla –

(TOM *is about to strike, but suddenly* MA *is between* TOM *and the* COP.)

MA   Tom! Stay put! Mister. They's people sleepin' here – what you doin'?

Cop	Just checkin' ma'am. Deputy sheriff ma'am.
Ma	I see – you got a tin button and a gun. But where I come from you keep your voice down. In my country you watch your tongue.
Cop	You ain't in your country now ma'am. This is my country and here we do what we want. (*A stand off for a few seconds while he squares up to* Ma. *He shines the torch squarely at* Tom.) If you're here this time tomorra I'll run you in.

(*They go. The family have all woken and are standing around.*)

Ma	Nearly hit 'im with a skillet. Ain't going to threaten my family like that. Now back to sleep. (Tom *comforts* Ma.) I pray God we get some res'. I pray Jesus we gonn' lay down in a nice place. I pray God we be let to wash some clothes. We ain't never been dirty like this. Don't even wash potatoes 'fore we boil 'em now.

(Granma *cries out again.* Ma *wearily goes to her.*)

Ma	Okay Granma, I'm a-comin'.

(Connie *and* Rose of Sharon, *in the dusk.*)

Rose of Shar.	Connie, talk about when we get there. So's I can sleep.
Connie	Well I'll get to studyin' nights right off. Gonna get one a them books that tells about it an' cut the coupon, send it right off.
Rose of Shar.	How long, you think?
Connie	How long what?

ROSE OF SHAR.	How long 'fore you'll be makin' big money an' we got ice? I want ice.
CONNIE	Can't tell. Can't really rightly tell. Fella oughta be studied up pretty good 'fore Christmus.
ROSE OF SHAR.	Soon's you get studied up we could get ice an' stuff, I guess.
CONNIE	What you gonna need ice roun' Christmus for?
ROSE OF SHAR.	I'd like ice any time. You'll get me ice – won't ya?

(*We hear* GRANMA's *voice and* MA *soothing.*)

MA	Alright. It's gonna be all right. Granma. You know the family got to get acrost. You know that.
UNCLE JOHN	(*from the darkness*) You all right?
ROSE OF SHAR.	You all right, Granma?
MA	Yeah. We're all right. Let's all get some sleep.

(*They settle for the night. A transition as the truck is packed and again repositioned. The company sing "Do Re Mi" by Woody Guthrie.*)

Lots of folks back east they say,
Leaving home everyday,
Leading the hot old dusty road,
To the California line.
Across the desert sands they go,
Heading for that old dust bowl,
Think they're going to a sugar bowl,
But this is what they find:
Now the police at the port of entry say
You're number 14,000 for today

If you ain't got the do ray mi folks,
You ain't got the do ray mi,

Well you'd better get back to Texas,
Oklahoma, Kansas, Georgia, Tennessee.
California is a Garden of Eden,
A paradise to live in or see,
But believe it or not,
You won't find it so hot,
If you ain't got the do ray mi.

Scene 8

Music underscores. The Jalopy travels.

CONNIE	Want to get there quick now.
UNCLE JOHN	Want to get there quick.
AL	Want to get there quick now.
MAN 9	250,000 people saying . . .
ALL	Want to get there quick now.
WOMAN 4	Wonder what it's like out there?
MAN 10	Well, the pitchers sure do look nice.
WOMAN 6	I seen one where its hot an' fine,
MAN 3	An' walnut trees an' berries;
MAN 8	An' right behind, close as a mule's ass to his withers,
WOMAN 6	They's a tall mountain covered with snow.
ALL	Want to get there quick.
UNCLE JOHN	If we can get work it'll be fine.
CASY	Won't have no cold in the winter.
WOMAN 5	Kids won't freeze on the way to school.
MAN 9	Getting there quick now –
ALL	Wanna get there quick.
AL	When you cross the Colorado river, there's the desert, they say.
MAN 9	Look out for the desert.
CONNIE	Yeah, look out for the desert.
MA	Yeah, look out for the desert.
UNCLE JOHN	See you don't get hung up.

WOMAN 5	Take plenty water, case you get hung up.
PA	Take her at night.
CASY	Yeah otherwise she'll cut the living Jesus outa you.
WOMAN 4	Get there however but get there quick!
ALL	Get there however but get there quick!
VOICES	(*singing, picking up the refrain*) If you ain't got the do ray mi folks, You ain't got the do ray me, Well you'd better get back to Texas, Oklahoma, Kansas, Georgia, Tennessee. California is a Garden of Eden, A paradise to live in or see, But believe it or not, You won't find it so hot If you ain't got the do ray mi.

Scene 9

Darkness. A flashlight. It is as if the truck has just been stopped.

OFFICER 1 (MAN 8)	Stop right there.
TOM	What's this here?
OFFICER 2 (MAN 10)	Agricultural inspection. We got to look over your stuff. Got any vegetables or seeds?
TOM	No.
OFFICER 1	Well, we got to look over your stuff. You got to unload. Come on.
MA	No, no, stop. Look, Mister. We got a sick ol' lady. We got to get her to a doctor. We can't wait. You can't make us wait.
OFFICER 1	Yeah? Well, we got to look you over. Unload.

MA	I swear we ain't got anything! I swear it. An' Granma's awful sick.
OFFICER 2	You don't look so good yourself.
MA	Look. Clear out everybody, let's have a little bit of respect. (*She draws the canopy back at the back of the truck. The* OFFICER *shines his torch in.*)
OFFICER 1	God, she is sick. You swear you got no seeds or fruits or vegetables?
MA	No, no. I swear it!
OFFICER 1	Then go ahead. You can get a doctor in Barstow. That's only eight miles. Go on ahead.
MA	Thanks Mister.

(*The* OFFICERS *come forward.*)

OFFICER 1	I couldn' hold 'em.
OFFICER 2	Maybe it was a bluff.
OFFICER 1	Oh, Jesus, no! You should of seen that ol' woman's face. That wasn't no bluff. Come on.

(*They walk away.*)

MA	I didn' wanta stop there, fear we wouldn' get acrost.
TOM	Yeah! But how's Gramna?
MA	She's awright. Now drive on. We got to get acrost. Come on.

(*They pile on the jalopy. A lone voice sings.*)

VOICE	Lots of folks back east they say Leaving home everyday

Leading the hot old dusty way
To the California line
Across the desert sands they roll
Heading for that old dust bowl
Think the're going to a sugar bowl
But this is what they find
Now the police at the port of entry say
You're number 14,000 for today

(*The music rises and the stage transforms into a great dawn. Slowly,* Tom *leading, they get down from the truck, seeing California ahead of them.*)

Woman 5   And then suddenly they see the great valley below them.

Tom   Stop! The desert's past! Pa, Al, Ma, for Christ's sake – the desert's past!

Al   Jesus Christ! Look!!

Woman 4   The vineyards, the orchards, the great flat valley, green and beautiful, the trees set in rows, and the farm houses –

Pa   God Almighty!

Woman 6   The distant cities, the little towns in the orchard land, and the morning sun, golden on the valley.

Al   Look at her!

Woman 5   The grain fields golden in the morning, and the willow lines, the eucalyptus trees in rows.

Pa   I never knowed they was anything like her.

Woman 6   The peach trees and the walnut groves, and the dark green patches of oranges. And red roofs among the trees, and barns – rich barns.

Al   Ma! Come look. We're there!

RUTHIE	It's California.
WINFIELD	There's fruit!
TOM	Where's Ma? I want Ma to see it. Look, Ma! Come here, Ma. (MA *clambers down slowly.*) My God, Ma, you sick?
MA	(*her voice a croak*) Ya say we're acrost?
TOM	Look.
MA	(*she looks*) Thank God! The fambly's here. The fambly's arrived!
	(*Her knees buckle and she sinks to the ground.*)
TOM	You sick, Ma?
MA	No, jus' tar'd.
TOM	Didn' you get no sleep?
MA	No.
TOM	Was Granma bad?
MA	I wisht I could wait an' not tell you. I wisht it could be all nice.
PA	Then Granma's bad.
MA	Granma's dead.
PA	When?
MA	Before they stopped us in the night. That's why I didn't want them to look. I was afraid we wouldn' get acrost, I tol' Granma we couldn' he'p her. The fambly had ta get acrost. I tol' her, tol' her when she was a-dyin'. We couldn' stop in the desert. There was the young ones an' Rosasharn's baby. I tol' her. She can get buried in a nice green place, trees aroun' an' a nice place. She got to lay her head down in California.

TOM	Jesus Christ! You layin' there with her all night long!
MA	The fambly hadda get acrost. (TOM *moves close to put his hand on her shoulder.*) Don' touch me. I'll hol' up if you don' touch me. That'd get me. I'm tar'd. I'm awful tar'd.
RUTHIE	Tha's Granma, in the back there an' she's dead.
WINFIELD	I seen her. She ain't breathin' at all. She's awful dead.
MA	It's purty, I wisht they could have saw it, Granpa and Granma.
PA	I wisht so too.
WOMAN 5	They looked down the mountain, twisting and looping, losing the valley sometimes, and then finding it again.
WOMAN 4	And the hot breath of the valley came up to them, with hot green smells on it, and with resinous sage and tarweed smells.
TOM	I guess we got to go to the coroner, wherever he is. We got to get her buried decent. How much money might be lef '?
PA	'Bout forty dollars.
TOM	Jesus, are we gonna start clean! We sure ain't bringin' nothin' with us! We sure ain't bringin' nothin' with us to California!

Scene 10

The company stand, motionless, spread out across the stage. A lone voice, joined by others as we crescendo.

	(*sung*) Yes I feel like travelling on,

(*sung*) Yes I feel like travelling on,
I feel like travelling on.
My heavenly home is bright and fair,
I feel like travelling on.

(*Voice and music continue to underscore.*)

AL There's thirty thousan' acres, out west of here. Just layin' there. Jesus, what I could do with that, what I could do with five acres of that.

ROSE OF SHAR. Well, it ain't ours, an' it ain't gonna be ours. That's owned. That ain't ours.

CASY Three hundred thousand people, hungry and miserable; if they ever know themselves, the land will be theirs and all the gas, all the rifles in the world won't stop them. Our people are good people; our people are kind people. Pray God some day kind people won't all be poor. Pray God some day a kid can eat.

(*sung*) Yes I feel like travelling on,
I feel like travelling on.
My heavenly home is bright and fair,
I feel like travelling on.

End of Act One

ACT TWO

Scene 11

The Joads are camped out in a crowded, filthy site. Throughout the scene as MA *prepares the food (stew), hungry kids pass and gather round.* RUTHIE *and* WINFIELD *bring some kindling over.*

RUTHIE (*sulkily*) This place ain't like you said. It's dirty.

MA It's only for a short while. Till we get work. Now sit down there and eat your stew, the men'll be back soon.

(*A young man,* FLOYD (MAN 8), *working on a car spare part, has been watching.*)

FLOYD You folks jus' come acrost?

TOM Yeah.

FLOYD Never been in Hooverville before? This here's her. Where all the bums live.

TOM We ain't no bums, we're lookin' for work. We'll take any kind a work.

FLOYD Yeah? What ya think ever'body else is lookin' for? Di'monds?

TOM Ain't they no work? This is California. We seen all this stuff a-growin'. We seen han'bills – orange ones. Says they need lots a people out here to work the crops.

FLOYD Sure. They say they's three hunderd thousan' us folks here, an' I bet ever' dam' fam'ly seen them han'bills.

TOM But if they don' need folks, what'd they go to the trouble puttin' them things out for?

FLOYD	Use your head, why don'cha? Look, s'pose you got a job a work, an' there's jus' one fella wants the job. You got to pay 'im what he asts. But s'pose they's a hunderd men. S'pose them men got kids, an' them kids is hungry. Suppose a lousy dime'll buy a box a mush for them kids. S'pose a nickel'll buy at leas' somepin for them kids. An' you got a hundred men remember. Jus' offer 'em a nickel an hour – why, they'll kill each other fightin' for that nickel. Hell, pay 'em fifteen cents. You can print a hell of a lot of han'bills with what ya save payin' fifteen cents, an hour.
TOM	But they is work, Christ Almighty, with all this stuff-growin' – orchards an' grapes. They got to have men. I seen all that stuff.
FLOYD	I tell ya, they's a big son-of-a-bitch of a peach orchard I worked in. Takes nine men all the year roun'. Takes three thousan' men for two weeks when them peaches is ripe. Whole part a the country's peaches. All ripe together. When ya get 'em picked, there ain't another damn thing in that part a the country to do. An' then them owners don' want you there no more. Three thousan' of you. The work's done. You might steal, you might get drunk, you might jus' raise hell. An' it's a pretty country, but you stink it up. They don' want you aroun'. So they kick you out, they move you along. That's how it is.
TOM	Them peaches got to be picked jus' when they're ripe, don't they? Well, s'pose them pickers got together an' says, 'Let' em rot.' Wouldn' be long 'fore the price went up, by God!
FLOYD	Weell, you figgered out somepin, didn' you? Come right outa your own head. Know what? The folks with the peach orchard figgered her out too. Look, if the folks gets together, they's a leader – got to be – fella that does the

	talkin'. Well, first time this fella opens his mouth they grab him an' stick 'im in jail. An' if they's another leader pops up, why, they stick 'im in jail.
TOM	I ain't gonna take it. Goddamn it, I an' my folks ain't no sheep. I'll kick the hell outa somebody.
FLOYD	Like a cop?
TOM	Like anybody.
FLOYD	You're nuts. They'll pick you right off. You got no name, no property. They'll find you in a ditch, with the blood dried on your mouth an' your nose. Be one little line in the paper – 'Vagrant foun' dead'. An' that's all. Don't hit no cops. That's jus' suicide. Be bull-simple – jus' play dumb all the time.

(*He walks away.* TOM *walks to where* MA *is making the stew.*)

MA	(*to the kids gathered round*) Lord God Almighty! Where'd you come from? Didn' you have no breakfast?
BOY	No, ma'am. They ain't no work hereabouts.
MA	Didn' none of you here have no breakfast? How long you been in California?
GIRL	Oh, 'bout six months. We lived in a gov'ment camp a while, an' then we went north, an' when we come back it was full up. That's a nice place to live, you bet.
MA	Where's that?
GIRL	Over by Weedpatch. Got nice toilets an' baths, an' you kin wash clothes in a tub, an' they's water right handy, good drinkin' water; an' nights the folks plays music an' Sat'dy night they give a dance.

MA	I never heard about it. I sure could use a wash tub, I tell you. Mus' cost a lot, I sure wisht we could go there. (*She looks at the children staring. Turns to* TOM.) I dunno what to do. I got to feed the fambly. What'm I gonna do with these here?
TOM	(*to the children*) You git. Go on, now, git. There ain't enough for you –
MA	I can't turn them away. Look. You little fellas go and get you each a flat stick and you can dip in a little. (*The kids race off and return during the scene and dip their sticks in.* ROSE OF SHARON *enters from the shelter.* CONNIE *appears.*)
CONNIE	You alright?
ROSE OF SHAR.	I oughta help Ma, but ever' time I stirred about I throwed up. Just sick all the time.
CONNIE	Fella says there ain't no work for miles around. If I'd of knowed it would be like this I wouldn't of came. I'd a studied nights 'bout tractors back home an' got me a three-dollar job. Fella can live awful nice on three dollars a day, an' go to the pitcher show ever' night, too.
ROSE OF SHAR.	You're gonna study nights about radios. (*There is a long pause.*) Ain't you?
CONNIE	Yeah, sure. Soon's I get on my feet. Get a little money.
ROSE OF SHAR.	You ain't givin' it up!
CONNIE	No – no – 'course not. But – I didn' know they was places like this we got to live in.
ROSE OF SHAR.	You got to!

CONNIE	Sure! Sure, I know. Got to get on my feet. Get a little money. Would a been better maybe to stay home an' study 'bout tractors. Three dollars day they get, an' pick up extra money, too. (*She looks hard at him.*) But I'm gonna study, soon's I get on my feet.
ROSE OF SHAR.	We got to have a house 'fore the baby comes. We ain't gonna have this baby in no tent!
CONNIE	Sure. Soon's I get on my feet. (*He walks away, angry and frustrated.*)

(PA, UNCLE JOHN, AL *and* CASY *arrive.*)

MA	Any luck?
PA	No. No work where we was lookin' anyways.
MA	Well come and get this. Take your plates. You children run along now. Hurry up.

(*The men take their food and settle, a little away from* MA.)

PA	We buried Granma nice – but now we only got a few dollars left. We got to find work!
AL	Fella says they's gonna be work up north. Place called Santa Clara Valley. Prune pickin', an' pears an' cannery work
TOM	How far?
AL	Says maybe two hundred miles.
PA	That's a hell of a long ways. How we know they's gonna be work when we get there?
AL	Well, they ain't nothin' here. Fella says we oughta get out in the night. Oughta get there an' get some work lined up.
TOM	Why we gotta sneak away?

AL	Says if ever'body gets there, ain't gonna be work for nobody.
TOM	It's jus' such a hell of a long ways.
PA	An' Ma – we . . . kinda hoped we could get work here an' rent a house to live in.

(FLOYD *wanders over.*)

FLOYD	Any luck?
UNCLE JOHN	There ain't a han' turn of work in the whole damn country.
AL	That's what I'm saying.
TOM	When is they gonna be work aroun' here?
FLOYD	Well, in a month the cotton'll start.
TOM	A month? With a few dollars left –
AL	So we move on –
PA	No, Al. Ma ain't a-gonna wanta move. She's all tar'd out.
AL	By God, I think I'll go that 200 miles myself.
PA	An' leave the fambly?
AL	Sure. I'd come back with my jeans plumb fulla jack. Why not?
TOM	Ma ain't gonna like no such thing.

(*A* WOMAN *approaches* (WOMAN 5), *with a young child in tow.*)

WOMAN	Afternoon.
MA	(*about to go in*) Afternoon. Can I he'p you in any way?
WOMAN	You kin he'p me by mindin' your own childern an' lettin' mine alone.

MA	I ain't done nothing.
WOMAN	My little fella jus come in smellin' of stew. You give it to 'im. He tol'me. Don'you go a-boastin' an' a-braggin' 'bout havin' stew. Don' you do it. I got 'nuf troubles 'thout that. Come in ta me, he did, an' says, "Whyn't we have stew?"
MA	Set down, set down an' talk a piece.
WOMAN	No I ain't gonna set down. I'm tryin' to feed my folks, an' you come along with your stew.
MA	That was 'bout the las' stew we're gonna have till we get work. S'pose you was cookin' a stew an' a bunch a little fellas stood aroun' moonin', what'd you do? We didn't have enough, but you can't keep it when they look at ya like that.
WOMAN	Good afternoon! (*The* WOMAN *goes.*)
MA	(*as the men stare at her*) I don't like this place. But we got stay. We got to find work!

(*A* MAN *in khaki trousers and a flannel shirt appears* (MAN 5), *as if from nowhere. He is the* CONTRACTOR.)

CONTRACTOR	You men want to work?
TOM	Sure we want to work. Where's the work at?
CONTRACTOR	Tulare County. Fruit's opening up. Need a lot of pickers.
FLOYD	You doin' the hiring?
CONTRACTOR	Well, I'm contracting the land.
FLOYD	What you payin?
CONTRACTOR	(*not enjoying being interrupted*) Well, can't tell – exactly – yet. Bout thirty cents, I guess.

FLOYD	Why can't you tell? You took the contract, didn't you?
CONTRACTOR	(*warily*) That's true. But it's keyed to the price. Might be a little more, might be a little less.
FLOYD	I'll go, Mister. You jus' show your licence, an then give us an order to go to work, and where, and when, an how much we'll get, and you sign that, an we'll all go.
CONTRACTOR	You telling me how to run my own business?
FLOYD	If we're workin' for you, it's our business too.
CONTRACTOR	Well, you ain't telling me what to do. I told you I need men.
FLOYD	You didn' say how many men, an' you didn' say what you'd pay.
CONTRACTOR	Goddamn it, I don't know yet.
FLOYD	If you don' know, you got no right to hire men.
CONTRACTOR	I got a right to run my business my own way. If you men want to sit here on your ass, okay. I'm out getting men for Tulare County. Who wants to work? Going ta need a lot of men.
FLOYD	(*a few men have moved forward*) Listen. Twice now I've fell for that. Maybe he needs a thousan' men. He'll get five thousan' there, an' he'll pay fifteen cents an hour. An' you poor bastards'll have to take it 'cause you'll be hungry. 'F he wants to hire men, let him hire 'em an' write it out an' say what he's gonna pay. Ast ta see his license. He ain't allowed to contract men without a license.
CONTRACTOR	Joe! (*The* DEPUTY SHERIFF (MAN 10) *appears.*) Ever see this guy before Joe? This one.

DEPUTY JOE   What did he do?

CONTRACTOR   He's talking red. Agitatin'. Ever see him before?

DEPUTY JOE   Seems like I have. Las' week when that used car lot was bust into. Seems like I see this fella hanging around. Yep! I'd swear it's the same fella. Get over there and get in that car.

TOM   You got nothin' on him.

DEPUTY JOE   If you'd like to go too, you jus' open your trap once more. They was two fellas hangin' around that lot.

TOM   I wasn't even in the State las' week.

DEPUTY JOE   Well, maybe you're wanted someplace else. You keep your trap shut.

CONTRACTOR   You fellas don't want ta listen to these goddamn reds. Troublemakers – they'll get you in trouble. Now I can use all of you in Tulare County.

DEPUTY JOE   Might be a good idea to go. Board of health says we got to clean up this camp. An' if it gets around that you got reds out here – why somebody might get hurt. That's just a friendly way of telling you might be a bunch a guys round here with pick handles, if you ain't gone.

CONTRACTOR   That's all. There's men needed in Tulare County. Plenty of work.

DEPUTY JOE   Yep. That's all. Hear what I'm, sayin'? I don't want one of you here by tomorra morning . . . (*To* FLOYD.) Now you get in that car –

(*Suddenly* FLOYD *spins and with one movement punches the* DEPUTY. *The* DEPUTY *staggers and*

> TOM *puts out his foot for him to trip over. The* DEPUTY *falls heavily and rolls, reaching for his gun. The* DEPUTY *fires from the ground. A woman in front of a tent screams as the bullet rips through her hand.* TOM *kicks the* DEPUTY *in the neck and then stands back as the heavy man crumples over. He is briefly unconscious. The* CONTRACTOR *has run off.* TOM *takes the man's gun and throws it to the side.*)

TOM Fella like that ain't got no right to a gun.

(CASY *moves close to* TOM.)

CASY You got to git out! Go inside an hide. He didn' see you kick 'im, but he seen you bowl him over. Quick. They'll fingerprint you. You broke parole. They'll send you back!

TOM Jesus! I forgot!

CASY Go quick, 'fore he comes to!

TOM Lemme get his gun –

CASY No. Leave it. Go!

(AL *steps over to the fallen* DEPUTY.)

AL Jesus, Tom sure flagged 'im down!

(*A siren in the distance.*)

CASY (*to* AL) Get out – go on. You don't know nothin'.

AL How 'bout you?

CASY Somebody got to take the blame I'll just sit in jail a while –

AL But . . .

CASY If you mess in this your whole fambly, all your folks, gonna get in trouble. Maybe they'll send Tom back to McAlester.

AL	Okay. I think you're a damn fool, though.
CASY	Sure, Why not?

(*The siren screams again and again, and comes closer.* CASY *kneels beside the* DEPUTY *and turns him over. The man groans, and* CASY *wipes the dust off his lips. A* DEPUTY (MAN 9) *armed with a rifle arrives, with the* CONTRACTOR.)

DEPUTY 2	What the hell's goin' on here?
CASY	I knocked out your man there. Well, he got tough an' I hit 'im, and he started shootin'. So I hit 'im again.
DEPUTY 2	Well, what'd you do in the first place?
CASY	I talked back. They's a woman down the row like to bleed to death from his bad shootin'.

(CONTRACTOR *goes off to look.*)

DEPUTY 2	We'll see about that later. Joe, is this the fella that hit you?
DEPUTY JOE	(*staring at* CASY) It don't look like him.
CASY	It was me, all right. You got smart with the wrong fella.
DEPUTY JOE	You don't look like the right fella to me.
CASY	I'll go without no trouble.
CONTRACTOR	(*coming from the woman's tent*) Jesus what a mess a .45 does make! They got a tourniquet on. We'll send a doctor out.
DEPUTY 2	Let's go.

(*They walk off with* CASY. AL *whistles for* TOM. *Gradually the family appears.*)

PA	Now what the hell made the preacher do that?
ROSE OF SHAR.	Where's Connie? Where'd Connie go?
TOM	Casy shouldn' of did it.
AL	Comes from bein' a preacher. They get all messed up with stuff.

(FLOYD *runs in, frantically packing his things.*)

FLOYD	You folks want some advice? Get out. They'll burn ya out if ya don't. The pool-room boys'll be down here tonight to burn us out.
TOM	Guess we better git, then. Where you a-goin'?
FLOYD	Why, up north. A fella tol' me 'bout a government camp near here. Go South on 99 and turn east to Weedpatch.
AL	I heard about it. Hot water and bath tubs.
FLOYD	Sure sounds nice. Treat ya like a man 'stead of a dog. Ain't no cops there. So long!
TOM	We got to get on. So long. (*To the family.*) We got to get outa here. You heard the fella, he says they'll burn the camp tonight.

(*Driving music. They pack the truck.*)

ROSE OF SHAR.	You seen Connie? Any one seen Connie?
AL	Yeah. I seen him. Way to hell an' gone up the river.
ROSE OF SHAR.	Was – was he goin' away?
MA	Rosasharn. What'd Connie say to you?
ROSE OF SHAR.	Said it would a been a good thing if he stayed home and studied up tractors.
PA	Tractors! Connie wasn' no good. I seen that a long time. No guts, jus' too big for his overalls. If he ain't no good, we don' want him.

TOM	We ain't sure he's gone for good. Maybe we'll meet up again. We got no time for talkin'. We got to get on our way.
MA	Come on!! We got to go quick.
PA	Come on John!
UNCLE JOHN	No. Go on all of you. Ain't goin'. Gonna res' here. No good goin' back. No. Ain't goin'.
TOM	Come on John. We can't go 'less you go!
UNCLE JOHN	Go ri-long. All of ya. I ain't no good. I ain't no good. Jus' a-draggin' my sins, a-dirtyin' ever'body.
TOM	Jesus – you got no more sin'n anybody else.
UNCLE JOHN	Nobody don' know my sins, nobody but Jesus. He knows. Ain't goin' go. Jus' tar'd. Gon' res' ri' here. Ri' here.
TOM	(*to* PA) He been drinkin?
PA	Ever since we got here.

(TOM *puts his fist against the point of* UNCLE JOHN's *chin. He makes a small practice arc twice, for distance, and then, with his shoulder in the swing, he hits the chin a delicate perfect blow.* JOHN's *chin snaps up and he falls backwards. They pile him into the truck.*)

(*Music sequence continues.* MA *walks over to* ROSE OF SHARON.)

MA	Come on, Rosasharn. We're a-goin.
ROSE OF SHAR.	I want Connie. I ain't a-goin' till he comes back.
MA	Come on, Rosasharn. Come on, honey.
ROSE OF SHAR.	I wanta wait.
MA	We can't wait!

| TOM | He'll find us. Don' you worry. He'll find us. Come on, Al!

(AL *and* TOM *pick up* ROSE OF SHARON *bodily and load her on the truck. The family pile on,* TOM *stands defiant in front of the truck.*)

| TOM | Al, take that there monkey wrench, jus' in case. If anybody tries to climb up, let 'im have it. Pa – you can reach over an' get the jack handle.

(*Music as the truck starts up agitated, violent.*)

| TOM | They comes a time when a man gets mad . . .

| MA | Tom – you tol' me – you promised me you wasn't like . . . You promised!

| TOM | I know, Ma. I'm a-tryin'. But them deputies – Did you ever see a deputy that didn' have a fat ass? An' they waggle their ass an' flop their gun aroun'. Ma if it was the law they was workin' with, why, we could take it. But it ain't the law. They're a-workin' away at our spirits. They're a-tryin' to make us cringe an' crawl like a whipped bitch. They tryin' to break us. Them sons a bitches. It's a helluva thing when the time comes when the on'y way a fella can keep his decency is by takin' a sock at a cop!

| MA | You promised!

| TOM | Jesus Christ, Ma, they're workin' on our decency!

| MA | You promised, Tom. You got to keep clear. Get in the truck. The famblys breakin' up. You got to keep clear.

(*Music as they reposition the truck. Suddenly a crowd of men swarm about the truck, armed with pick handles and shotguns.* TOM *steps down.*)

Tom	Anythin' wrong?
Vigilante 1/ Woman 6	Where you think you're goin?
Tom	Well – (*And then his voice takes on a servile whine.*) We're strangers here, we heard about they's work in a place called Tulare. You don't happen to know –
Vigilante 2/ Man 9	Well, goddamn it, you're goin' the wrong way. We ain't gonna have no goddamn Okies in this town.
Tom	Which way is it at, Mister?
Vigilante 1	You head north. An' don't come back till the cotton's ready.
Tom	Yes, sir. (*They go and he gets back in the car.*) The sons-of-bitches.
Ma	You done good. You done jus' good. Now we got Uncle John in the back but we lost Connie. No matter – gotta' keep on. Gotta' try and keep the family together.
Tom	(*looking back*) We ain't goin' north. Goin' south. We couldn' let them bastards push us aroun'. Couldn'. Gonna look for that gov'ment camp. A fella said they don' let no deputies in there. Ma – I got to get away from 'em. I'm scairt I'll kill one.
Ma	Easy, Tom. Easy, Tommy. You done good once. You can do it again.
Tom	Yeah, an' after a while I won't have no decency lef'!

Scene 12

The company cover the stage. A vocal sequence, angry and bitter, underscored with music. Voice distribution as appropriate. During this sequence the Weedpatch camp is built.

MAN 8	The moving, questing people are migrants now.
WOMAN 6	The people are changed.
WOMAN 3	The children without dinner changed them.
PA	The endless moving changed them.
ALL	Migrants.
AL	And the migrants stream in on the highways and their hunger is in their eyes, and their need is in their eyes.
WOMAN 3	They have no argument, no system, nothing but their numbers and their needs.
UNCLE JOHN	Hey! If that fella'll work for thirty cents, I'll work for twenty-five.
MAN 10	If he'll take twenty-five, I'll do it for twenty.
MAN 5	No, me, I'm hungry. I'll work for fifteen.
TOM	I'll work for food.
MAN 9	Me. I'll work for a little piece of meat.
WOMAN 5	And this was good, for wages went down and prices stayed up.
ROSE OF SHAR.	The great owners were glad and they sent out more handbills to bring more people in.
WOMAN 5	And wages went down and prices stayed up.
MAN 4	And still the roads crowd with men ravenous for work.
AL	Murderous for work.
UNCLE JOHN	And the companies work at their own doom and they do not know it.

MA	The great companies do not know that the line between hunger and anger is a line.
ALL	The line between hunger and anger is a line.
WOMAN 3	And the anger begins to ferment.

Scene 13

The family have arrived in Weedpatch. MA is setting out their things. AL is working on the truck. Four ladies from the camp committee appear – JESSIE, ANNIE, ELLA and IVY – WOMEN 3, 4, 5 and 6.

IVY	Mrs Joad, ain't it?
MA	Yes –
ALL	Welcome to Weedpatch!
IVY	We are the Ladies' Committee . . .
ANNIE	Of Sanitary Unit . . .
ALL	Number Four.
MA	Pleased to be here – it's a nice place –
ELLA	We'll, that's because we're a government camp.
ANNIE	With wash tubs, running water . . .
IVY	Toilets and showers . . .
ALL	A camp committee . . .
JESSIE	And no cops.
AL	No cops, you said?
ANNIE	No cops.
IVY	We got our own cops. Folks here' their own cops.

JESSIE	No, sir. No cop can come in here without a warrant. They don't get in here.
ELLA	Some nights the boys patrol the fences, 'specially dance nights.
AL	(*who has wandered over*) Dance nights? Jesus Christ!
IVY	We got the best dances in the county every Saturday night. Got a dance tonight mat'r fact –
AL	Well, for Christ's sake! I'm gonna take a look aroun'!
JESSIE	We just came over see how you was, Mrs Joad. And set out the rules.
IVY	Mrs Bell?
JESSIE	Yes, Mrs Littlefield?
IVY	I'm chair this week, remember.
JESSIE	Oh sure, Mrs Littlefield.
IVY	So the rules, Mrs Joad is –
JESSIE	Til next week, when I'm –
IVY	Well you wait till next week then Mrs Bell. We exchange over every week, Mrs Joad. Till then I'm elected unanimous, aint that right?
OTHER TWO	That's right, Mrs Littlefield.
ANNIE	When you're knowed, Mrs Joad, maybe you could be 'lected to the committee – even one day become chair . . .
IVY	The rules, Mrs Joad. Costs a dollar a week, but you can work it out, carrying garbage, keeping the camp clean-stuff like that. The committee makes the laws. What they say goes.

JESSIE	But you can vote 'em out jus' as quick as you vote 'em in.
IVY	That's right, Mrs Bell. You can vote them out as quick as you can vote them in.
MA	It's so clean.
ANNIE	We all keep it that way.
ELLA	We got sub committees.
JESSIE	We take pride in Unit Number Four!
IVY	(*intimately*) We got our trouble with toilet paper, Mrs Joad. See, the whole camp chips in –
MA	Yes –
JESSIE	But Number Four is using more'n any other –
MA	No –
LADIES	Ahhuh!
ANNIE	It'll come up in the general ladies meetin', Mrs Joad.
IVY	I got a idea for a little bell that rings ever' time a roll turns over –
ALL	Then we could count how many everybody takes –
IVY	You sing, Mrs Joad? You wait till the women go a washin'. We have a chorus.
JESSIE	Singin' and washin the clothes all in time.
IVY	Ready girls? You pitch it up, Mrs Allen.

(*They sing, in four parts.*)

Beneath the cross of Jesus
I fain would take my stand.
The shadow of the mighty rock

Within a weary land.
A home within the wilderness,
A rest upon the way,
Beneath the cross of Jesus
Until my dying day.

(RUTHIE *and* WINFIELD *come running in.*)

RUTHIE	Ma! Winfiel', he bust a toilet.
WINFIELD	She pee'd in one!
MA	Now tell me what you done –
RUTHIE	It was a-hissin' and a-swishin . . .
MA	Show me what you done –
WINFIELD	I didn' kick it or nothin' – I jus' had a hol' of this handle here an' all the water come . . .
MA	(*laughing*) Thats the way she works, when you finish, you push that.

(*The committee ladies have witnessed this.*)

JESSIE	Sweet.
IVY	They ain't never seen real toilets before?
MA	(*defensively*) Course they have. But they was Oklahoma toilets, not California ones. They's a different action to 'em.
IVY	Welcome to Weedpatch, Mrs Joad! (*They go.*)
MA	Thank you very much.

(ROSE OF SHARON *enters, all scrubbed up.*)

ROSE OF SHAR. I jus' had me a bath! I was in there when a lady come in. An' that lady – she seen me an' she seen about the baby, an' – know what she said? Said they's a nurse comes ever' week. An' I'm to go see that nurse an' she'll tell me jus' what to do so's the baby'll be strong. An'

– know what? Las' week they was a baby born an' the whole camp give a party, an' they give clothes, an' they give stuff for the baby –

(*The men come over, washed and clean.*)

AL What a place! Know what a fella's doin'? He's buildin' a house trailer. Right over there, back a them tents. Got beds an' a stove, ever'thing. Jus' live in her. By God, that's the way to live! Right where you stop – tha's where you live. And there's a dance tonight –

MA I rather have a little house. Soon's we can, I want a little house.

PA First thing tomorra morning, Al, you an' me an' Uncle John'll go out looking for work. Who was them ladies?

MA (*daintily*) Jus' the Ladies' Committee – jus' come to see's we's alright. Jus' come over to invite your Ma to be on the committee sometime – that's all! Look at us! Where's Tom?

TOM (*appearing*) Here. Got up early and – well – found a coupla days work. Not much – laying pipes for a fella – payin' thirty cents an hour.

PA Thirty cents –

TOM It's work. Coupla days, he says. Good fella.

MA Look at us – clean and scrubbed and Tom got a whiff of work and we only been here a coupla hours! Praise God, we come home to our own people! These folks is our folks – is our folks. Them ladies they come over an' set an' says, "Mrs. Joad" this, an' "Mrs. Joad" that – an' "How you gettin' on, Mrs. Joad?" Why, I feel like people again. Right, we're all goin to the store. I want beans an' sugar an' a piece of

	fryin' meat. An' get somepin nice – anything, but nice – for tonight.
PA	But Ma, we only got a few dollars left!
MA	Tonight – we'll have – somepin nice. Then we'll go to the dance. I feel like people again!

(MA, PA, ROSE OF SHARON *and* KIDS *leave.* AL *takes* TOM *and* UNCLE JOHN *aside.*)

AL	Tom, Uncle John – been talking to some of the fellas here. They heard about how some agitator took a swipe at a deputy at that squatters camp we was at. They say there's always red agitators just before a pay cut. Contractors don't like government camps – want to get a deputy in here and clean us out.
UNCLE JOHN	They figure folks in the camp get used to being treated like humans, huh?
TOM	Aint no cops allowed in government camp, don't worry –
AL	But if there was a big fight and maybe shooting – a bunch of deputies could go in and clean out the camp. Do you know what I mean? Like if townsfolk were to come to the dance tonight. That's what they're sayin –
UNCLE JOHN	Put the word around.

Scene 14

The whole company begin to gather on stage. Violins, guitars, etc, appear.

WOMAN 6	Welcome to Weedpatch and the Saturday night dance. Come on in all and you townsfolk. Let's have a dance!

(*The scene explodes into a dance, furious and energetic. Some of the men are standing guard, including* Tom. *At a certain point two men* (Man 4 *and* 10), *obviously together, step onto the floor and create an incident. Immediately all the company, including the children, surround the three so that they are immobile. A hammering and whistling from the "entrance".*)

Man 5 — Open up. We hear you got a riot in there!

Uncle John — We got no riot, mister. We're just taking a rest between dances – isn't that right, boys?

Man 5 — Open up – we gotta come in and put that riot down –

Pa — What riot? Who are you?

Man 5 — Deputy sheriffs.

Tom — Got a warrant?

Man 5 — We don't need a warrant if there's a riot.

Al — Well, we got no riots here. Just a couple of – uninvited guests who just asked to leave. Isn't that right boys? Off you go.

(*The group slowly parts and walks the two men across the space. All very dignified and peaceful. Just before they leave,* Uncle John *turns to them.*)

Uncle John — Why do you do it boys? Deputy paid you to break up our dance – make a riot – why'd you do it?

Man 4 — Well, goddamn it, a fella got to eat.

Uncle John — Don't knife your own folks. We're tryin' to get along, havin' fun an' keepin' order. Don't tear all that down. You're jes' harmin' yourself.

(*They start to go.*)

TOM Le's jes' take a little swipe at 'em. Jes' one nice little swipe.

UNCLE JOHN No Tom! (*To the two men.*) Listen, you, we're lettin' you off this time. But you take back the word. If'n ever this here happens again, we'll jes' natcherally kick the hell outa whoever comes; we'll bust ever' bone in their body. Night all.

(*Gang members leave.*)

UNCLE JOHN Now let's dance

(*The music strikes up again and the whole community join the dance, which builds to a thrilling climax.*)

(*The music then changes to a minor tone, and underscores the next scene.*)

Scene 15

The family are sitting around the camp. The rest of the ensemble begin to watch them, and then turn to the audience.

MAN 9 Dancing is one thing. Eating is another.

WOMAN 5 Using up the valuable gas that they cannot replace, the men move along the beautiful roads, past orchards where the peaches were beginning to color.

WOMAN 3 Past vineyards with the clusters pale and green, under lines of walnut trees whose branches spread half across the road.

PA They's boun' to be work when them fruits gets ready.

AL	Ever' time the same: "No help wanted". "No trespassing".
UNCLE JOHN	Funny how they tell ya they ain't no work 'fore you ask 'em.
PA	Nothing.
AL	Like huntin' skunks under water.
WOMAN 4	The spring is beautiful in California. Valleys in which the fruit blossoms are fragrant pink and white waters in a shallow sea.
MAN 8	The men of science have done good work to perfect the seeds, the roots.
MAN 5	The men of chemistry have done good work to make sprays against pests, diseases and rot.
WOMAN 6	So the whole of California swells with excess.
WOMAN 5	And now the fruits of the vine and trees must be destroyed to keep up the price.
MAN 9	Or just left to rot.
WOMAN 3	The decay spreads over the State, and the sweet smell is a great sorrow on the land.
WOMAN 4	So men with hoses squirt kerosene on the surplus oranges and peaches.
MA	One month we been here, an' Tom had five days work.
WOMAN 6	And they dump potatoes in the rivers and place guards along the banks to keep the hungry people from fishing them out.
MA	One day more grease an' two days flour an' six potatoes. Look!

Man 5	There is a crime here that goes beyond denunciation. There is a failure here that topples all the successes of science.
Woman 4	Since children are dying because a profit cannot be taken from an orange.
Pa	Maybe we got to move on. We don't want to. It's nice here, an' folks is nice.
Ma	Well, if we got to, we got to. Now pack up! I ain't watching us starve. One day more grease an' six potatoes. Pack up!
Man 8	And in the eyes of the people there is the failure; and the eyes of the hungry there is a growing wrath.
Pa	We got hot water an' toilets –
Ma	Pa! We can't eat no toilets. Pack up!
Pa	Where we going?
Uncle John	Feller says they's peaches a-comin' in up north, near a place called Bakersfield.
Al	That'll take the last drop of gas –
Ma	Then that's where we'll go. We'll go now. I tol' you what's lef'.
Uncle John	If we're going, I'm going to get one last good crap before we go. These here nice toilets gets me sinful.
Ma	John! Get in that truck!
Uncle John	Right –
Pa	Seems like times is changed. Time was when a man said what we'd do. Seems like women is tellin' now. Seems like it's purty near time to get out a stick!

MA	You get your stick, Pa. When they's food an' a place to set, then maybe you can use your stick . But you ain't a-doin' your job, either a-thinkin' or a-workin'. You jus' get you a stick now an' you ain't lickin' no woman; you're a-fightin' her, 'cause I got a stick all laid out too.
PA	Now it ain't good to have the little fellas hear you talkin' like that –
MA	You get some bacon inside the little fellas 'fore you come tellin' what else is good for' em! Now get going, all of you! I ain't watching us starve!
WOMAN 5	In the souls of the people the grapes of wrath are filling and growing heavy, growing heavy the vintage.
MA	I ain't watching us starve!

Scene 16

Music. Travelling music, which mixes in with the sounds of a disturbance – the pickets are shouting. Amongst the noise they "arrive" (truck repositioned) and set up camp again. The BOOK KEEPER (WOMAN 3) *arrives with buckets. The family line up.*

BOOK KEEPER	Ever pick peaches before?
TOM	No ma'am. What was all the fuss at the gate, all the shouting?
BOOK KEEPER	That's not your affair. Can all of you work?
MA	(*pointing to* ROSE OF SHARON) Not her, she's due.
TOM	I didn't get an answer, ma'am. Why did it take four cops to get us through?

BOOK KEEPER	Got a little trouble, that's all. Stay out of it if I was you. Wages five cents a box. Pick careful. No bruised fruit. No windfalls. Bruise your fruit and we won't check 'em. There's your buckets.
TOM	Fulla holes on the bottom.
BOOK KEEPER	Sure. That keeps people from stealing them. Get going.
TOM	They don't waste no time.
PA	Come on, let's get to work! I told you we'd find work if we looked hard enough! Look at us!
TOM	(*to* AL) I don't like it. Them was our people at the gate, all yellin'. I'm going to take a look around later.

(*The men and kids go off to pick.*)

MA	That's better. With five of us a-workin maybe I can get some credit at the store right off. First thing I'll get is some milk, cause you need that. And soap. Gotta have soap. Why, if we pick plenty peaches we might get a house. We got to have a house. (*To* ROSE OF SHARON.) You'll be alright here, alone, if I go pickin'?
ROSE OF SHAR.	I'm alone anyways ain't I?

(*Before* MA *leaves, a* WOMAN (WOMAN 6) *passes.*)

MA	Afternoon.
WOMAN	Howdy. You just in?
MA	Yes ma'm. Goin' pickin'. Five of us.
WOMAN	All you pickin' you'll soon get a dollar's worth.
MA	Yes, ma'm. I'll be straight to the store.

ACT TWO

WOMAN	To the company store. With a slip for a dollar.
MA	Yes ma'am!
WOMAN	Where you can get a twelve cent loaf for fifteen cents.
MA	Excuse me?
WOMAN	Shop man'll tell you. If you don't like it go into town and spend a gallon on gas, he'll say. They got you both ways roun'. And remember, you ain't got your dollar cash. All you got is credit, which you gotta spend in their shop, at their prices.
MA	But who's they?
WOMAN	Same people who owns them peaches. Same people who give you a dollar credit.
MA	But that means . . .
WOMAN	Like I says – got you both ways roun'. Good luck.

(MA *goes.*)

ROSE OF SHAR. You ain't seen a man name of Connie Rivers? Aint heard of no Connie Rivers?

WOMAN No, ma'am, I aint.

ROSE OF SHAR. (*alone on the truck*) Ain't anybody heard of Connie Rivers?

(*Music.*)

Scene 17

Darkness. Distant shouting. A figure (TOM) *moving about. A* GUARD (MAN 10) *appears.*

Guard 1	Who's there?
Tom	Got a place where a fella can take a bath, mister?
Guard 1	Well, there's a hose over there.
Tom	Any warm water?
Guard 1	Say, who in hell you think you are, JP Morgan?
Tom	No. No, I sure don't. Good night, Mister.
Guard 1	Not that way. Stay away from the fence. Them crazy pickets might get you.
Tom	What pickets?
Guard 1	Them goddamn reds. There's goin to be a mess tonight. Stay away.

(Tom *goes but waits in the dark. A* Second Guard (Man 8) *appears.*)

Guard 2	S'matter, Mack?
Guard 1	Why, them goddamn Okies. Is they warm water? he says.
Guard 2	Prob'ly been in a gov'ment camp. We ain't gonna have no peace till we wipe them camps out.

(*They go.* Tom *in the shadows again. A fence. He climbs. A group of shadows.*)

Tom	Evenin'.
Man 4	Who are you?
Tom	Well – I guess, well – I'm jus' goin' past.
Man 4	Know anybody here?

Tom	No. I tell you I was jus' goin' past. (Tom *sees* Casy.) Casy! Casy! For Chris' sake, what you doin' here?
Casy	Why, my God, it's Tom Joad!
Man 4	Fellas, shh! Know him, do ya?
Casy	Know him? Christ, yes. Knowed him for years. I come west with him. Well, for God's sake! Where's your folks? What you doin' here?
Tom	Well, we heard they was work this-a-way. An' we come, 'an a bunch a State cops run us into this here ranch an' we been a-pickin' peaches all afternoon. I seen a bunch a fellas yellin', so I come out here to see what's goin' on. Casy – you done your time?
Casy	Sure. I'm an old jailbird. Like you.
Tom	I never forgot what you did for us.
Casy	You been pickin'? They let you in?
Tom	What's goin' on?
Casy	Maybe I can't tell you. Maybe you got to find out. This here is a strike see.
Tom	Strike?
Casy	We all heard about the work here. There was a hell of a lot of us. They says it's gonna be five cents. We start workin' and then' they says they're payin' two-and-a-half cents. A fella can't even eat on that, and if he got kids – so – we says we won't take it. So they drove us off. An' all the cops in the worl' come down on us. How much they payin' you?
Tom	Five cents.

CASY
: Five cents. They'll soon drop to two-and-a-half again. Tell your folks to come out.

TOM
: Pa wouldn' do it. I know 'im. He'd say it wasn't none of his business.

CASY
: Yes. I guess that's right. Have to take a beatin' 'fore he'll know. Lemme tell you somethin'. Jailhouse is a kinda funny place. They was nice fellas there, see. What made 'em bad was they needed stuff. An' I begin to see, then. It's need that makes all the trouble. One day they give us some beans that was sour. One fella started yellin', an' nothin' happened. He yelled his head off. Then another fella yelled. Well, sir, then we all got yellin'. And we all got on the same tone, an' I tell ya. By God! Then somepin happened! Trusties come a-runnin' and they give us some other stuff to eat – give it to us. All the voices shoutin' as one. Ya see! Tom, you do what you can and the only thing you got to look at is that everytime you take a step forward she may slip back a little but she never slips clear back and that makes everything alright.

MAN 4
: (*who has been listening out*) Goddamn it, I don't like it. Seems like I hear somepin, an' then I listen an' they ain't nothin' to hear.

CASY
: You're jus' jumpy. All of 'em's itchy. Them cops been sayin' how they're gonna beat the hell outa us an' run us outa the county. They figger I'm a leader 'cause I talk so much.

MAN 4
: They's somepin. I'm sure – Yeah, I hear it.

(*In the darkness a group of figures, townspeople, armed with pick handles.*)

TOWNMAN 1/ MAN 5
: That's him. That shiny bastard. That's him!

(*Figures approach* CASY, *very menacing.*)

CASY	Listen. You fellas don,' know what you're doin'. You're helpin' to starve kids.
TOWNMAN 1	Shut up, you red son-of-a-bitch.
CASY	You don' know what you're a-doin'.
TOWNMAN 1	I said shut up!

(*A swing of a pickaxe handle and* CASY *hits the ground. A beat.*)

TOWNMAN 2/ MAN 9	Jesus, George. I think you killed him!
TOWNMAN 1	Put the light on him. Serve the son-of-a-bitch right.

(*Suddenly* TOM *leaps forward and grabs the pickaxe handle and floors the man with a heavy blow to the head. Shouts, running, moving figures, fighting, confusion.*)

Scene 18

We see TOM *making his way to the Joad place. He has a rag to his face.* MA *wakes.*

MA	Tom, what's the matter?
TOM	Sh! Don't talk loud. I got in a fight.
MA	Tom!
TOM	I couldn't help it, Ma.
MA	You in trouble?
TOM	Yeah. I got to hide.

(RUTHIE *comes out.*)

RUTHIE	What's the matter'th him, Ma?
MA	Hush. Go wash up.

RUTHIE	We got no soap.
MA	Well, use water.
RUTHIE	What's the matter'th Tom?
MA	He's hurt. An' don't you tell nobody. (*To* TOM.) Is it bad?
TOM	Nose busted.
MA	I mean the trouble?

(*Others wake, appear.*)

AL	Well, for Chris' sake! What happened to you?
UNCLE JOHN	What's the matter?
PA	What the hell is this?
MA	(*to* RUTHIE) Will you go wash your face!
TOM	No. They got to hear. They got to know. They might blab if they don't know. I went out to see what all the yellin' was about. An' I come on Casy.
PA	The preacher?
TOM	Yeah the preacher. Only he was leadin' the strike. They come for him.
PA	Who?
TOM	Some guys with pick handles. They killed him. Busted his head. I went nuts – grabbed the handle. I – clubbed a guy.
PA	Kill him?
TOM	I dunno. Tried to.
PA	Was you saw?
TOM	I dunno.

UNCLE JOHN	Casy – he was a good man. What'd he want to mess with that stuff for?
TOM	They came to work for five cents a box.
PA	That's what we're gettin'.
TOM	Yeah. We was breakin' strike. They lowered it to two-and-a-half cents.
AL	You can't eat on that.
TOM	Says now they've bust the strike we'll get two-and-a-half cents.
AL	Why the sons of bitches.
PA	Jesus. We got to know, Tom – think you killed this fella?
TOM	I hope so. I hope I killed the bastard.
MA	Tom! Don't talk like that. Ruthie, if anybody asks you – Tom is sick – you hear? If you tell, he'll be sent to jail – you hear? Why'd they kill him, Tom?
TOM	He says to them "You got no right to starve people. You don't know what you're doin' ". Then they hit him and I hit them.

(*Voices off. A commotion. The men run out.*)

MA	It's awright. I wisht you didn' do it. I wisht you wasn' there. But you done what you had to do.
TOM	Ma, I'm a-gonna go away tonight. I can't go puttin' this on the family.
MA	Tom! Goin' away ain't gonna ease us. It's gonna bear us down. We're family – and I'm tryin' – all the time – to keep us family whole

and clear. I can't get straight. Seems now we ain't clear no more. They ain't nothin' keeps us clear. We're crackin' up, Tom. There ain't no fambly now. And Rose – she gonna have her baby an' they won't be no fambly. I don' know. I been a-tryin' to keep her goin'. Winfiel' – what's he gonna be, this-a-way? Gettin' wild, an' Ruthie too – like animals. Got nothin' to trus'. Don' go, Tom. Please don't go.

(*Men come in, except* AL. *Voices from outside.*)

BOOK KEEPER   (*off stage*) House twenty-five. Number's on the door.

MAN 5   (*off stage*) Okay Mister. Whatcha payin'?

BOOK KEEPER   (*off stage*) Two-and-a-half cents.

MAN 5   (*off stage*) Why, goddamn it, a man can't make his dinner!

BOOK KEEPER   (*off stage*) That's what we're payin'. There's two hundred men coming from the South that'll be glad to get it.

TOM   Jus' like Casy said!

(UNCLE JOHN *has fetched* WINFIELD, *who is sick.*)

UNCLE JOHN   The little fella's purty weak. Looks like he got worms.

MA   He ain't fevered. But he's white and drawed out. I know. He's hungered. Got no strength. I got him a can o' milk but he won't drink it.

(MA *fetches a small can of milk and sets it by* WINFIELD. PA *looks at it.*)

PA   Christ Awmighty! We all need stuff. Now why' he have to get sick?

MA	I don't know why, but he is. Now jus' you sit quiet. We got to figger. Winfiel', here, drink this.
WINFIELD	I can't. I'd sick it all up.
UNCLE JOHN	He can't take it now, Ma. Wait a little.
MA	Alright. Don't none of you touch that. That's for Winfiel'.
ROSE OF SHAR.	I ain't had no milk. I oughta have some.
MA	(*bearing up*) I know that honey, but you're still on your feet. This here little fella's down.

(AL *comes back in, very agitated.*)

AL	Tom, looks like you done it.
TOM	I kinda thought so.
AL	People ain't talkin' 'bout much else. They talking getting a posse an' they's fellas talkin' up lynchin' –
TOM	I done it – but I only after they killed Casy. He was a Good man. Goddamn it. I can't get that picture outta my head, him layin there, head crushed flat – oozing.
AL	That ain't the way they're tellin' it now. They're sayin' the other fella done it fust. An' – the way I heard it, they think the fella got hit. They think – his face –
MA	Oh Tom!
TOM	Easy, Ma. I got to go. Get outa here.
MA	You ain't goin'. We're a-takin' you. We're movin' on.
PA	But –

MA	You listen! Now, I got it figgered out. We'll put one mattress on the bottom in the back, an' then Tom gets quick in there, an' we take another mattress so it makes a cave, an' he's in the cave.
PA	But Ma –
MA	Don't argue. That's what we'll do.
PA	Seems like the man ain't got no say no more. Come time we get settled down, I'm a-gonna smack her.
MA	Come that time, you can. Roust up!

(*They pack the truck, this time with an aching slowness despite the urgency as the movements we know so well are repeated.*)

MA	Quick now. Git that mattress in! Tom, you jump up there an' git under. Hurry up. Wherever we get to, we'll find him a creek where he can hide till his face gets well. Come on!

Scene 19

They pile on once again with driving, angry music.

ROSE OF SHAR.	Feel bad all a time. Wisht I could set still in a nice place. Wisht we was home an' never come. Connie wouldn'a went away if we was home. He would a studied up an' got someplace.
MA	(*to* AL) Know where we're a-goin'?
AL	No – jus' goin', an' gettin' goddamn sick of it.
ROSE OF SHAR.	I ain't so tur'ble far from my time. They better be a nice place for me. I ain't had milk like

	they said I ought. If Connie hadn' went away, we'd a had a little house by now, with him studyin' an' all. Would a got milk like I need. Would a had a nice baby. This here baby ain't going to be no good. I ought a had milk.
	(She reaches into her apron pocket and puts something into her mouth.)
MA	What you eatin'?
ROSE OF SHAR.	Nothin' – just a piece a chalk.
MA	Why that's just like eatin' dirt.
ROSE OF SHAR.	I feel like I wan' it. Got no husban', got no milk.
MA	If you was a well girl I'd take a whang at you. Right in the face. Come on now! All of you!
RUTHIE	They gonna have croquet where we're goin'? I like the croquet.
MA	I don't know!
ROSE OF SHAR.	There'd better be a nice place!
	(They try to quiet ROSE OF SHARON'S *moaning.* MA *explodes.)*
MA	You listen y'all! I'm gonna' tell ya. In a little while it ain't gonna' be so bad. In a little while. Now come on! Dear Jesus, I hope it's awright. I hope this is goin' to be alright.
	(The music swells. During the following sequence a boxcar camp is created and the truck unloaded once more.)

Scene 20

WOMAN 5	Cotton Pickers Wanted.

Woman 4	Here, up this road.
Man 8	Like to get our hands on the bolls.
Pa	I'm a good picker.
Man 5	Got a bag?
Pa	Well, no, I ain't.
Man 5	Cost ya' a dollar, the bag.
Man 4	Bet I could pick cotton if I was blind. Got a feelin' for a cotton boll.
Al	Cotton pickin's good work.
Woman 6	Heard 'bout the cotton-pickin' machine?
Al	Yeah.
Woman 6	If it comes – it'll put han' pickin' out.
Woman 5	Now, fill up the bag 'fore dark. Wise fingers seeking in the bolls. Hips hunching along, dragging the bag.
Woman 3	Kids are pickin' too, tired now in the evening.
Man 4	Wisht it would last. It ain't much money. God knows, but I wisht it would last.
Man 9	If they was only fifty of us, we could stay awhile, but they's five hunderd. She won't last hardly at all.
Man 5	Winter's comin' fast. They ain't no work at all in California in the winter.
Pa	They say a thousan' men are on their way to this field. We'll be fightin, for a row tomorra. We'll be snatchin' cotton, quick.
Man 8	Cotton Pickers Wanted.

Scene 21

The boxcar camp, broken down boxcars, families settled in them. MA *with* ROSE OF SHARON.

MA (*bearing up, it's a terrible place*) It's nice. It's almost nicer than anything we had 'cept the gov'ment camp.

ROSE OF SHAR. I miss the government camp.

MA We'll get better'n that in time. You see. We been real lucky. Got floor – an' roof. Can' imagine a better place for you to get him bore. Come on, out my way now. (ROSE OF SHARON *groans.*) You alright?

(*The men return from the fields.*)

MA How's the pickin?

PA We're doin' fine. We made three and a half today.

(AL *moves over and joins a girl in one of the other cars.*)

AL Ma – me 'n Aggie's going to walk awhile.

(*They go off.*)

PA Look at him – moment we're off the field he only got eyes for one thing –

MA Went to the shop. Got some pork chops. An' a nice piece a boilin' beef. An' milk an' potatoes. Look at us!

UNCLE JOHN Funny thing. Now I got a little bit, I wanta buy stuff. Stuff I don't need. Like to git one a them safety razors. An' I don't need no safety razor, neither. Had a beard for forty years. Stuff settin' out there, you jus' feel like buyin' it whether you need it or not.

PA	Getting thirsty, John? Jus' wait til the cotton's done. Then you can go on a hell of a drunk.
UNCLE JOHN	I'm alright right now. I'm working hard and sleepin' good. No dreams or nothin'.
MA	How much cotton's left? Pa? How much cotton is there?
PA	Hard to tell. Le's jus hope it don't rain. If it rains –

(*A beat.*)

MA	You alright?
PA	Just tard. That's all.
MA	Well, I gotta go and see Tom. Take some food, see how he is.
PA	I don't like to think of him out there hidin' in the bushes.
UNCLE JOHN	He got to – till his face mends.
MA	He's gonna have a scar too –
UNCLE JOHN	Hell, everybody got scars.

(WINFIELD *enters, agitated.*)

WINFIELD	Ma.
MA	What?
WINFIELD	Ma – Ruthie tol'.
MA	Tol' what?
WINFIELD	'Bout Tom.
MA	What! Who to?
WINFIELD	Well, she only tol' a little bit – she was eating her chocolate bar and a big girl come up and

took it and hit Ruthie a big one. So then Ruthie cried, an' she said she'd git her big brother, an' he'd kill that big girl. An' that big girl said, 'Oh, yeah?' An she hit her again. Then – an' then, Ruthie said our brother already killed two fellas. An' – an' – that big girl said, 'Oh, yeah! You're jus' a little smarty liar'. An' Ruthie said, 'Oh, yeah? Well, our brother's a-hidin' right now from killin' a fella, an' he can kill that big girl's brother too' . . .

MA You git and tell Ruthie to shut her mouth. Oh my – oh my dear sweet Lord Jesus asleep in a manger! What we goin' to do now? I'm going to see Tom – got to see Tom!

(*She goes.*)

Scene 22

Darkness. MA *calls softly for* TOM.

MA Tom, oh, Tom!

TOM (*Appearing from the gloom*) That you, Ma?

MA Right over here.

TOM How is everybody?

MA We made purty good – and your brother Al met a real nice girl an' – Tom – where are you?

TOM Right here, Ma.

MA Let me touch you. It's like I'm blin'. I want to remember – even if it's only my fingers that remember. You got to go away Tom. Tom – Ruthie told about you.

TOM Ruthie – what for?

Ma	Well, it wasn' her fault. Got in a fight, an' says her brother'll lick that other girl's brother. An' she tol' that her brother killed a man and was hidin'.
Tom	That's jus' kids' talk, Ma.
Ma	Them kids'll tell it aroun' and then when the folks'll hear, they liable to get men out to look, jus' in case. Tom, you got to go away. I been squirrelin' money away. Hol' out your han', Tom. I got seven dollars here.
Tom	I ain't gonna take ya money. I'll get 'long all right.
Ma	Tom, I ain't gonna sleep none if you got no money.
Tom	I ain't gonna take it.
Ma	Tom, you got no right to cause me pain. You take it. You hear me?
Tom	Alright. Ma, I remember somethin' the preacher said to me. I want to tell you now. Goes, "Two are better than one, because they have a good reward for their labor. For if they fall, the one will lif' up his fellow, but woe to him that is alone when he falleth, for he hath not another to help him up".
Ma	Yeah? Go on, Tom.
Tom	"Again, if two lie together, then they have heat: but how can one be warm alone? And if one prevail against him, two shall withstand him, and a three-fold cord is not quickly broken".
Ma	An' that's Scripture?
Tom	Casy said it was.
Ma	Tom, what you aimin' to do?

Tom	I been thinkin' how it was in that gov'ment camp, how our folks took care a theirselves, an' they wasn't no cops wagglin' their guns, but they was better order than them cops ever give. I been a-wonderin' why we can't do that all over. Throw out the cops that ain't our people. All work together for our own thing – all farm our own lan'.
Ma	So – what you gonna do?
Tom	What Casy done.
Ma	But they killed him!
Tom	Yeah. He didn' duck quick enough. He wasn' doing nothin' against the law, Ma. I been thinkin' a hell of a lot, thinkin' about our people livin' like pigs, an' the good rich lan' layin' fallow, or maybe one fella with a million acres, while a hunderd thousan' good farmers is starvin'. An' I been wonderin' if all our folks got together an' yelled, like them fellas yelled –
Ma	They'll drive you, an' cut you down –
Tom	They gonna drive me anyways. They drivin' all our people.
Ma	You don't aim to kill nobody, Tom?
Tom	No. I been thinkin', long as I'm a outlaw anyways, maybe I could. Hell, I ain't thought it out clear, Ma. Don' worry about me now. Don' worry about me.
Ma	How'm I gonna know 'bout you? They might kill ya an' I wouldn' know. They might hurt ya. How'm I gonna know?
Tom	Well, maybe like Casy says, a fella ain't got a soul of his own, but on'y a piece of a big one – an' then –

MA	Then what, Tom?
TOM	Then it don' matter. Then I'll be all aroun' in the dark. I'll be ever'where – wherever you look. Wherever they's a fight so hungry people can eat, I'll be there. Wherever they's a cop beatin' up a guy, I'll be there. Why, I'll be in the way guys yell when they're mad an' I'll be in the way kids laugh when they're hungry an' they know supper's ready. An' when our folks eat the crops they raise an' live in the houses they build – why, I'll be there. See? God, I'm talkin' like Casy. Comes of thinkin' about him so much. Seems like I can see him sometimes.
MA	Tommy – I knowed from the time you was a little fella – they's some folks that's jest theirself and nothin' more. But you – everythin' you do is more than you. You're spoke for.
TOM	Now you better go.
MA	An', Tom, later – when it's blowed over, you'll come back. You'll find us?
TOM	I will. Till then, jes take ever' day.
MA	Tom, we're the people that live. They ain't gonna wipe us out. We go on. Don't you fret none – a different time's comin'. There's a different time a comin'.
	(TOM *has gone.* MA *turns to go back. A* MAN (MAN 5) *appears in the darkness.*)
MAN	Evenin'.
	(*Sound of thunder.*)
MA	Looks like we might have a little rain.
MAN	I hope not. Stop the pickin'. Lord knows, we need the pickin'.

Scene 23

A crack of thunder. Rain. The company stand in the rain on stage.

WOMAN 5	For two days the earth drinks the rain, until the earth is full. Then in the low places little lakes form in the fields.
MAN 5	The muddy water creeps up the banks until at last it spills over, into the fields, into the orchards, into the cotton patches where the black stems stand.
MAN 4	The little eddies wash out and the water comes inside, and the streams wet the beds and the blankets.
WOMAN 4	The people sit in wet clothes. They set up boxes and put planks on the boxes. Then, day and night, they sit on the planks.
WOMAN 3	And gradually they come to know the greatest terror of all.
MAN 5	They ain't gonna be no kinda work for three months.
WOMAN 6	And the rain falls steadily.
MAN 8	Then groups of sodden men go out, their clothes slopping rags, their shoes muddy pulp.
MAN 4	They splash out through the water, to the towns, to the country stores, to the relief offices.
MAN 9	To beg for food, to cringe and beg for food, to beg for relief, to try to steal, to lie.
WOMAN 5	And under the begging, and under the cringing, a hopeless anger begins to smolder. And in the little towns pity for the sodden men

	changes to anger, and anger at the hungry people changed to fear of them.
WOMAN 4	Then sheriffs swear in deputies in droves, and orders are rushed for rifles, for tear gas, for ammunition.

(*A shot rings out.*)

WOMAN 3	The coroners were not too busy. The coroners' wagons backed up through the mud and took out the dead.
MAN 8	No work till spring. No work.
MAN 9	If no work, no money – no food. Nothing.

Scene 24

In the boxcar camp. The rain falls.

MA	You alright?
PA	Look at that rain. Spen' all my time a-thinkin' how it use' ta be. Spen' all my time thinkin' of home, an' I ain't never gonna see it no more.
MA	Can't think of home, Pa. This here's purtier – better lan'. Only regular work we need and then –
PA	I know. But I don't see it, thinkin, how the willow's los' its leaves now. Sometimes figgerin' to mend that hole in the south fence. Funny! Woman takin' over the fambly. An' I don' even care.
MA	Woman can change better'n a man. Woman got all her life in her arms. Man got it all in his head. Always thinking.
PA	Git so I hate to think. Goin' back to a ol' time to keep from thinkin'.

UNCLE JOHN	I can't think at all. Don't seem like I'm hardly awake no more.
PA	Look at that rain. Seems like our life's over an' done.
MA	(*sternly*) No, it ain't. It ain't, Pa, John. An' that's one more thing a woman knows. Man, he lives in jerks – woman, it's all one flow, like a stream, its like the the river, it goes right on. We ain't gonna die out. People is goin' on – changin' a little, maybe, but goin' right on.
PA	How can you tell? What's to keep all the folks from jus' gittin' tired an' layin' down?
MA	Because we got to go on. Ever'thing we do – is aimed right at goin' on. Jus' try to live the day. (PA *begins to cry softly.*) Jus' live the day. Don' worry yaself.
PA	They might be a good year nex' year.
MA	Yes . . .
PA	Back home.
AL	(*appearing with* AGGIE (WOMAN 6).) Water's risin'. She's risin' fast.
	(ROSE OF SHARON *comes out of the boxcar and suddenly falls to the ground.*)
MA	Rosasharn? You alright? You got a chill. This here girl ain't well. What's the matter? Your time come? You got a pain?
ROSE OF SHAR.	No, jus' don' feel good. Jus' feel bad – cover me up, I'm cold.
MA	Get a blanket, someone!
RUTHIE	(*coming to* MA) Wassa matter wi' her?
MA	She's sick –

RUTHIE	I'm hungry.
MA	No, you ain't. You had good mush.
RUTHIE	Wisht I had a box a Cracker Jack. There ain't nothin' to do. Ain't no fun.
MA	They'll be fun, you jus' wait. Be fun purty soon. Git a house an' a place, purty soon.
WINFIELD	Wisht we had a dog.
MA	(*with great effort*) We'll have a dog; have a cat too. Don't bother me. Rosasharn's sick. They'll be fun. In a little while!

(ROSE OF SHARON *cries out.*)

MA	What is it? Help, someone!
MRS WAINWRIGHT/ WOMAN 5	Want help?
MA	Look! I think it's come. It's early.
MRS WAIN.	Well, she oughta be up on her feet. Oughta be walkin' aroun'.
MA	She can't. She ain't got the strength. (*To the* KIDS.) Rosasharn gonna have her baby.
RUTHIE	I wanta watch, Ma. Please let me.
MA	Ruthie! You git now. You git quick.
MRS WAIN.	Aggie!
AGGIE	Yeah, Ma?
MRS WAIN.	You take these two over to our place. The girl's time's come!

(AGGIE *takes the* KIDS *away.*)

MA	Pa! Her time's come.
PA	Then we better build a bank – or the water'll come at us. Al – we got to build a bank!
AL	Need more'n us – be a lotta work and she might come over anyways.
PA	We got to buil' that bank – your sister's time's come. (*To other men, shouting into the void.*) Anybody? We got to build a bank here. Stop the water. My girl got her pains. We can't go now.
MAN 9	It ain't our baby.
MAN 8	Come on – this man's family goin' to have a baby. Let's help!
MAN 9	Won't do no good. Water's gonna come through no matter how high we build her!

(*Screams from inside the car.*)

AL	She's risin', look, she's risin'!
UNCLE JOHN	(*who can take no more*) Hell, I'll build her all by myself! I can't stand that yellin'! Give me shovel there!

(*He moves off the boxcar. Screams come from inside. AL and PA frantically restrain UNCLE JOHN, struggling with the shovel.*)

PA	You take it easy. You'll kill yaself!
UNCLE JOHN	I can't he'p it. I can't stan' that yellin'. I can't stand it.
PA	But jus' take it easy!
UNCLE JOHN	By God I'll hold that water back myself. Jus stop that screaming!

(*Screams from inside the boxcar. There is a crash and the men freeze.*)

MAN 5	Then, from up the stream a ripping crash, a great cottonwood toppling. The men stop to watch.
WOMAN 3	The branches of the tree sink into the water and edge around with the current. Slowly the tree edges down the stream.
MAN 9	The men watch. The tree moves slowly towards them. And very slowly the tree swings around. The water piles up behind. The tree moves and tears the bank apart.
AL	The truck!
	(AL *runs for the truck. He turns the engine, but nothing, only a hoarse whisper. Silence. The men stand around in the rain, their faces blank and forlorn.* MA *comes out with a little bundle.*)
MA	Never breathed. Never was alive.
PA	(*totally defeated*) We done what we could.
MA	I know.
PA	Thank she's gonna be all right?
MA	I dunno.
PA	Well – couldn' we of did nothin' more?
MA	No. They was on'y one thing to do ever – an' we done it
AL	Truck is flooded.
MA	I know.
PA	You know ever'thing.
	(*A long pause.* MRS WAINWRIGHT *comes out.*)
MA	You been frien'ly. We thank you.

MRS WAIN.	No need to thank. S'pose we was down. You'd a give us a han'.
MA	Yes, we would.
MRS WAIN.	Or anybody.
MA	Or anybody.

(*The family stand around in the rain, purposeless, defeated. A kind of listless hopelessness pervades.*)

MA	Could one of you fellas take this and bury it?
PA	'Gainst the law to bury it.
MA	They's lots a things 'gainst the law that we can't he'p doin'.
UNCLE JOHN	I'll do it, sure I will. Come on, give it to me. Come on! Give it to me.

(*He takes the dead baby.*)

Gonna' set you in the water. Gonna send you down stream to the town so's you can tell 'em. Go down in the street an' rot an' tell 'em that way. That's the way you can talk. Don' even know if you was a boy or a girl. Go on down now, an' lay in the street an rot. Maybe they'll know then.

(*He exits with the bundle. The rain beats down and they listlessly stare at it.*)

PA	Ma? Did we slip up? Is they anything we could of did?
MA	Don't take no blame. Hush! It'll be awright.
PA	Maybe the water'll go down and then maybe we'll be able to move on.
MA	No. We gotta' get outa here now – get to higher ground.

Pa	We can't.
Ma	It's time for it. Al – we got to go, come on.
Al	Ma, I ain't goin'. I'm staying with Aggie here. We figgers to get married and I'm gonna git a job in a garage – and rent a house for a while and . . .
Pa	Now you just . . .
Al	We are, and there aint nobody gonna stop us!
Pa	Ma!
Ma	We're glad Al. We're awful glad. You take care of the stuff. If Tom comes – tell him we'll be back. Tell him be careful. When the water goes down – why, we'll be back. Pa. Come on, Rosasharn. We're going to a dry place. Git your back bent, Pa.

(Pa *slips as it were into the water and stands waiting.* Ma *helps* Rose of Sharon *down from the platform and steadies her.* Pa *takes her in his arms, holding her as high as he can, and pushes his way carefully through the deep water, to a higher level.* Uncle John *returns and carries* Ruthie *and follows.* Winfield *sits on* Ma's *shoulder.*)

Ma	Climb on my shoulder – there! Now, keep your feet still.

(*They move off. The stage clears completely to a wide open space.*)

Scene 25

Pa, Ma, Uncle John, *carrying* Rose of Sharon, Ruthie *and* Winfield, *trudge the stage in the rain. Eventually* Ma *sees a barn. As they move towards it, it is created on stage. In it, two figures, a boy and a sick man* (Man 4 *and* 10).

MA	(*they enter the barn*) They's hay. Come on in, you. Lay down, Rosasharn, lay down an res'. I'll try to figger some way to dry you off.
RUTHIE	Ma! Ma!
MA	What is it? What you want?
RUTHIE	Look! Over there.
	(*The two figures sit in the gloom; the man lying on his back, and the boy sitting beside him, his eyes wide, staring at the newcomers.*)
MA	You own this here?
BOY	No, jus' come in outa the wet.
MA	We got a sick girl. You got a dry blanket we could use an' get her wet clothes off?
	(*The boy hands her a ragged blanket.*)
MA	Thankya, what's the matter'th that fella?
	(*The boy speaks in a croaking monotone.*)
BOY	First he was sick. Now he's starvin'.
MA	What?
BOY	He ain't et for six days.
MA	Your pa?
BOY	Yeah. Las' night I went and bust a window an' stole some bread. Made him chew her down. But he puked it all up, and then he was weaker. Got to have soup or milk. You folks got money to get milk?
MA	No. Don' worry. We'll figger somethin' out.
BOY	He's dyin' I tell you! He's starvin' to death.
MA	Hush. We'll figger somethin' out.

(*A sense of knowing spreads across her face and she turns to* ROSE OF SHARON, *who connects deeply with her. For a moment the two women communicate silently.*)

ROSE OF SHAR.   Yes, I will.

MA   I knowed you would. I knowed!

ROSE OF SHAR.   Will you all – go out?

(*The others leave the space,* ROSE OF SHARON *offers her breast to the starving man.*)

You got to. There. There.

(*As the man takes her breast, the closing music begins to swell.* MA *steps forward.*)

MA   There was a time when we was on the lan'. And we were one with the lan'. They was a boundary to us then. Ol' folks died off, an' little fellas came, and we was always one thing – we was the family, whole an' clear. We did what we could. You do what you can. Preacher said, you do what you can, an' the only thing you've got to look at is that every time we take a step forward she may slip back a little – but she never slips clear back. An' that makes the whole thing right. "Two are better than one, for how can one be warm alone. And if another prevails against them, two shall withstand him. Two are better than one, for if they fall, the one will lift up his fellow. But woe to him that is alone when he falleth, for he hath not another to help him up".

(*The music draws to a conclusion.*)

The End.

Down In The River

Trad. arr. Dyfan Jones

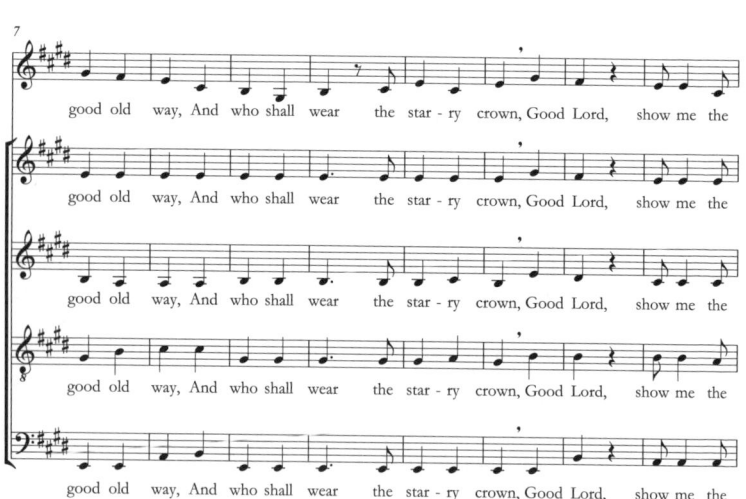

© Copyright 2006 by Dyfan Jones
PHOTOCOPYING THIS COPYRIGHT MATERIAL IS ILLEGAL

Act One – Scene 5
Page 27

My Heavenly Home
(*Granpa's burial*)

Trad. arr. Dyfan Jones

My Heavenly Home

Trad. arr. Dyfan Jones

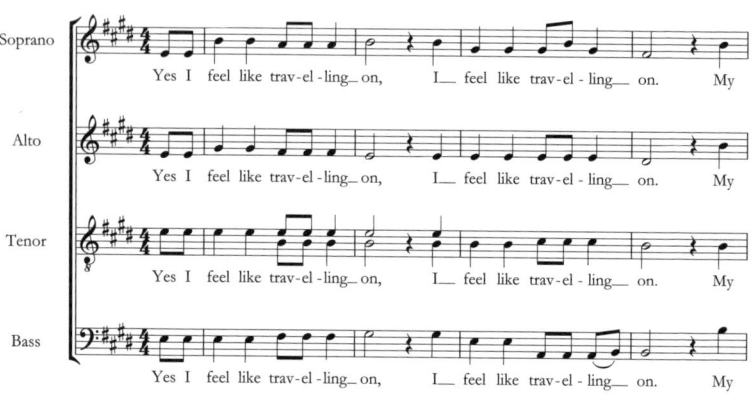

© Copyright 2006 by Dyfan Jones
PHOTOCOPYING THIS COPYRIGHT MATERIAL IS ILLEGAL

Beneath The Cross
(Ladies)

Composed and arranged by
Dyfan Jones

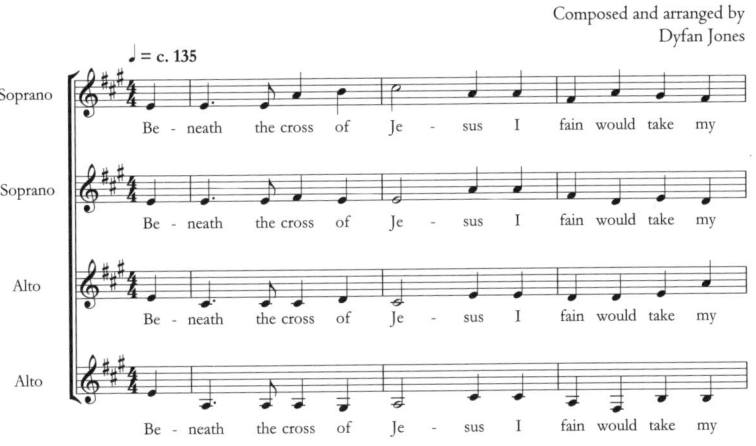

© Copyright 2006 by Dyfan Jones
PHOTOCOPYING THIS COPYRIGHT MATERIAL IS ILLEGAL